LIFE AND HOW TO LIVE IT

REMEMBERING MIKE ADAMS

I will write a book—it will be called
"Life and How to Live It"
~ R.E.M. ~

(Mike's favorite band in his college years)

COMPILED AND NARRATED BY

DAVID ADAMS

Ballast Books, LLC
www.ballastbooks.com

ISBN: 978-1-955026-56-7

Printed in Hong Kong

Published by Ballast Books
www.ballastbooks.com

For more information, bulk orders, appearances, or speaking requests,
please email: info@ballastbooks.com

CONTENTS

I Mike Adams am a boy
of The Law I Think That I am
a very wise person and cops are
a very good frend of me I Think
I will Do my very best to fight wi
The badge on my chest.

cop of
The Law

I am a brave
man and good.

Mike was, as you will soon learn, "a brave man and good."

INTRODUCTION

Mike's favorite story about me—his older brother, David—is that when we were kids, I would get exasperated with him and I would say, "Mike, stop being such a smart aleck. What are you going to do when you grow up? You can't be a professional smart aleck!" Then, years later, he started getting paid for his satirical and irreverent articles and speeches, which did, in fact, make him a "professional smart aleck," as he enjoyed reminding me.

So, okay, Mike always was a bit of a smart aleck. You could say that he was always a free speech advocate, even before he had ever heard of the Bill of Rights! This was Mike's lifelong character trait, and there were other recurrent ones, such as his intelligence, his wit, and his ability to build and maintain relationships.

But there were also some major transformations in his life. In fact, this book is primarily the story of a man transformed.

- *Academically, from a D student to an A student*
- *Spiritually, from an atheist to a Christian*
- *Politically, from liberal to conservative*
- *Morally, from pro-abortion to anti-abortion*
- *Socially, from private citizen to public figure*

In the first section of this book, "Learning," we will follow Mike's life journey and see how and why these transformations occurred.

The second section, "Teaching," is about Mike's passion for helping others and for sharing what he learned—not just book learning but also life experiences.

The third section, "Reflecting," as the name implies, shifts the focus to Mike's reflections on his life and on some of the lives lost.

The last section, "Extra Credit," is a miscellany for further reading and insight.

This book is based primarily on my favorite columns Mike wrote about his life. Since he never finished writing his life's story, I would like to start off with some background, and as we go along, I will try to piece it all together into what I hope will be a fitting tribute.

For our first Christmas without our parents (2019), Mike and I wanted to take a trip down memory lane to the old neighborhood where we grew up, Clear Lake City, a suburb of Houston located next to NASA's Johnson Space Center, where our parents worked. (Mike and I were born in Mississippi and briefly lived in New Orleans and Fort Worth before settling in Houston in 1969, when Mike was four years old.)

We drove and walked around and saw many familiar sights, such as our old house, our old playground, and our old ballfield. But while many things had remained the same, much had changed. For example, the single-screen movie theater—where we had seen Patton, Planet of the Apes, 2001: A Space Odyssey, *and countless other movies—had been torn down and replaced with a convenience store.*

We attended the Christmas service at our old church—University Baptist Church—where we saw some old family friends and chatted briefly with the (relatively) young man running the audio/video, the son of another boy who had lived on our street in the seventies. Back then, we were just kids, mind you, and even though we went to church, little did we know what the Lord was raising us up to do.

By 1970s standards, we enjoyed a basic middle-class lifestyle. We were not rich, but that did not seem to bother us. Our annual vacation was a trip to see our grandparents on my mother's side in Gulfport, Mississippi, a six-hour drive on the new Interstate I-10. Mike and I enjoyed many wonderful experiences there and had happy memories of visits with friends and family.

Twice we managed to save enough money to drive all the way to Los Angeles to see my dad's mother and stepfather. Unlike the trip to Gulfport, from which I recall endless boring hours of driving through swampland, the drive to LA was a great adventure through the expansive American Southwest with memorable stops, such as Carlsbad Caverns, White Sands, the Painted Desert, and most notably, the Grand Canyon, along the way. We all especially loved the Grand Canyon, but it made a huge impression on Mike. In fact, he made several return visits as an adult, and his Facebook profile picture was often a photo of him at that amazing natural wonder.

Later, references to the American Southwest would keep popping up in his writings. Here are some examples:

"There is a real understated beauty throughout the plains of northern New Mexico. She's like that girl in home room that you never really noticed until your senior year."

"Summer road trip fever resumes tomorrow. Friday road trip to Santa Fe, New Mexico. Saturday to Albuquerque, NM.

Sunday, Painted Desert, Arizona. Monday, Four Corners, Utah. Tuesday, back speaking at Summit in Colorado."

"Another day older and another day closer to retirement in Arizona."

I could write at great length about these road trips, but, simply put, these journeys were very meaningful to us and showed us that there are parts of America that are imperfect, flawed, and ugly—but also that we still live in a great and beautiful nation that is worth loving and fighting for. The desire to fight for a better America drove Mike for the rest of his life.

As I write this, I am sorely missing Mike and am thinking about how I would love to reminisce with him again and how I wish he were writing this book instead of me, especially as he always had a great memory for details. When we lost him, we also lost so many stories… I feel compelled to preserve the stories that he did leave behind.

When Mike passed in 2020, I knew that I wanted to publish a book that would honor him, preserve his memory, and pass along his wisdom and unique insights. I also wanted to make readers laugh, since humor was such an important part of Mike's life. He was always laughing and making others smile or laugh, too.

Initially, I thought I would choose Mike's best columns— no easy task, since he wrote about 1,200 of them during his career! This would be his "Greatest Hits," so to speak. And yes, that would have made a good read and worthy tribute. But I quickly realized that most of my favorites were autobiographical in nature—seemingly random stories about his friends, family, and life experiences, especially from his "Life and How to Live It" series—and that arranging those in chronological order could create a nearly complete biography. Almost an autobiography, if you will.

I have added my commentary in order to fill in the gaps, add context, and share my insights. For the sake of clarity, my comments and observations will be in italics like this, while Mike's words and those of other contributors will not.

It is my hope that you will enjoy this book and gain a deeper understanding and appreciation of who he was and why he was loved and followed by so many people.

PART ONE

Learning

The Three Pirates, Mike, Jim, and Scott, all grown up.

Me sitting in Mike's car, taking a picture of the school on what would be his last visit there and the last time I hung out with him.

CHAPTER 1

~⌒~

Three Pirates Look at 40

Originally published in 2004.

Mike and I were nearly polar opposites. I'm an introvert and, growing up, I mostly kept to myself. Mike, however, was always very sociable and funny. He had no trouble making and keeping friends. Here, he writes about his two oldest friends.

I will never forget the day I met Jim Duke. We were waiting in line to use the restroom at G.H. Whitcomb Elementary School in Clear Lake City, Texas. Well, that isn't exactly true. We were actually waiting in line in a contest in the boy's bathroom. We were both trying to be the first second-grader in school history to actually use the bathroom over the urinal, despite the fact that it was about six feet wide. We had been drinking water all morning long. Jim and I have always been ambitious.

That contest was interrupted when an emergency landed one of the contestants in an ambulance. I won't describe what happened after one boy held it in too long. Besides, I was in the stall trying to convince Jim that the first 'o' in the "Fort

Howard" label on the toilet paper dispenser was really an "a." We still argue about it to this day. Jim and I have always been intellectuals.

When Scott Maxson moved to town two years later, Jim and I got over our grammar school foolishness. In other words, we started acting like bona fide juvenile delinquents. I wasn't there the day that Jim and Scott lit the ditch on fire behind Scott's house, but I do remember hearing the sirens when the fire department arrived.

Nor was I there the time that Scott and Jim used tin foil to make fake nails that stuck out of the cracks in the street in front of Scott's house. It was pretty funny, until the guy in the El Camino truck (or was the El Camino a car?) spun out of control trying to swerve out of the way of the 'nails' in the road. I was also glad I wasn't there when he hopped out of that El Camino and chased them through the neighborhood.

I should be careful about making fun of Jim. He knows that I once got arrested at a party with a sixteen-year-old girl. Every time I try to defend myself by pointing out that I was only seventeen at the time, he talks about the second time I got arrested. That was after I relieved myself on the side of a car. I didn't know that it was an undercover cop car. And I sure didn't know that there were two undercover cops inside the car at the time. Come to think of it, I don't think my parents ever found out about it. I hope they aren't still reading my columns.

When these things come up, Scott never comes to my defense. When he tells the story about a bunch of guys beating me up in a parking lot when I was seventeen, he leaves out the part about him running away crying just minutes before (this account may not be entirely accurate, by the way). But he likes to remind me of the time I threw him in a pool at a party on his first date with Stephanie. He got me back later, when he stuffed a chicken breast under the carpet inside my 1970 GTO. By the time I went on a date with Amy four nights later, that chicken breast smelled pretty rotten. I thought I had just run over a possum or a raccoon. All night, Amy kept asking me why my car smelled so bad. We never went out again.

Of course, I got Scott back later when he was out on a date with a girl from Austin, Texas. I called and left a message calling myself 'Fabian' saying "Remember me? We met at a gay bar last Thursday night. Thanks for the back massage" before I hung up laughing. Scott was dumb enough to play his messages later that night when he took the girl home to his apartment. He spent the rest of the night convincing her it was just a joke. It was okay, though. They ended up dating for two years. We all laughed about it later. I get messages from "Fabian" to this day.

Eleven years later, Scott planted the 'men seeking men' section of the local personals under the passenger side visor of my car. Tandy found it on our second date. She also found the *Playgirl* centerfold he planted in my Pottery Barn catalog. When I was single, I always tried to put something on the coffee table that my dates would enjoy reading. That was going a little too far.

When I look back on endless nights of drag racing and burying that GTO speedometer at 140 mph, I feel lucky to be alive. The most dangerous thing Jim ever did until then was to get into a fistfight with a bush. The bush won, as I remember.

Whenever we get together, we talk about the good times. Not the time that Bubba was stabbed at the drive-in movie theater. Not about the times that weren't so good or the things that really hurt. Not the lies we told or the promises we broke.

We just think back to the promises we kept; the promise never to grow old and the promise never to stop laughing. And, above all, never to let old friendships die.

Old friends are blessings from God. And so are fortieth birthdays. Happy Birthday, Jim.

When Mike passed, Jim and Scott were still two of his best friends and served as pallbearers.

Mike was a loyal friend to many, and anyone who actually knew him, loved him. Relationship building is a lifelong endeavor—and Mike had mastered that art.

Mike also once said: "I caught up with an old friend tonight. We've been friends since 1972. This is the first time in a decade that one of our phone conversations was over in less than two hours. My advice is simple. Hang on to your old friends and make time for them, regardless of what life is throwing at you. When you talk with old friends, you realize that your present troubles are often meaningless. Keep focused on an eternal perspective. Never let it go."

From the 1983 Clear Lake High School yearbook.

Parked in front of our house.

CHAPTER 2

My 1970 GTO

Originally published in 2009.

This book opens with stories that are light-hearted and funny and show that Mike was a great person to be around. But we will see that Mike's stories were not just for idle entertainment, as he was often trying to make a point. Feedback from his students included comments on how they liked Mike's stories and how he used life experiences to get his points across in class.

For example, here is an actual test question that once appeared on his Introduction to Criminal Justice final exam:

Towards the end of the semester, I told you the story about my dog Rusty and his tendency to dig holes in the yard in the middle of the night. I also told you about my father's strategy of beating him with a newspaper the following morning. What was the moral of the story?

    a.   Punishments should be prompt
    b.   Punishments should be severe

c. Punishments should be certain
d. Punishment is ineffective

But I am getting ahead of myself.

In the summer of 1980, I was looking forward to turning sixteen and getting a driver's license. All my friends were looking forward to driving, but none as much as me. My friends would be driving used Mazdas and Toyotas that got good gas mileage. But my dad bought me a 1970 GTO. He didn't care that it got nine miles to the gallon. It looked like it was going thirty miles an hour when it was just sitting in the driveway.

Even though that old GTO was fast, it had worn hydraulic lifters that were sucking away horsepower and badly wearing down the stock Pontiac cam shaft. Nonetheless, I put the pedal to the floor and burned rubber every chance I got – that is, as long as the Houston Police were nowhere in sight.

One night on Highway Three, I began to hear an unfamiliar sound just after I floored the accelerator. I didn't realize it at the time, but I had merely dented the flywheel cover running over something in the road. But the sound it was making – coupled with the fact that it started just after I hit the accelerator – made me think I had spun a bearing on the crank shaft.

So, Dad and I went into the garage and pulled out the motor. After it was secure on the engine lift, we could see the source of the noise. And we knew we could just pull off the flywheel cover and hammer out the dent to fix the problem. But we also knew it would be so much more fun to rebuild the old motor. My dad must have figured that if I was going to finish at the bottom of my class academically,

I might as well have the fastest car among the 3300 students at Clear Lake High School.

For weeks, after I got home from school – and my dad got home from work – we toiled away on that engine. First, we started with the internal restoration. A Crane Blazer camshaft was the first high-performance extra installed. That went with new rings and bearings, new lifters, and a nice valve job on 10-to-1 heads with 2.11-inch intake valves.

Then, we got to all the really unnecessary aftermarket items. A Holly double pump carburetor sat on a new Edelbrock manifold. Headmond headers ran just below the stock chrome valve covers. We topped it off with a small chrome air filter that allowed people to better see what we had beneath the hood (plus, you could hear it sucking in air from inside the passenger compartment). Finally, there were nice Thrush mufflers to let people know we were coming long before we got there.

When we were done, my friend Jim Duke joked that he hoped his dad would hurry up and have a midlife crisis—so he could build him a hot rod, too. My buddy Terry Cohn said I had the coolest dad in town. Terry has always been wise beyond his years.

That GTO had other benefits, too. The first time I asked Jane out on a date, she said she'd go because she heard I had a cool car. When I picked her up, she said "This is it?" She was disappointed that it wasn't much to look at. But after I laid waste to a few Corvettes and Trans Ams, she changed her mind.

Those nights in Houston were legendary. Like the time I buried the speedometer at 140 on Interstate 45 on the way to Galveston. Or the time I beat James Armand's 1970 Camaro in a race up Falcon Pass. That night, I took everyone's money on the Clear Lake High School soccer team. Those were the days.

But my reign as the king of Falcon Pass would end in less than a year. Billy Peters had a cool dad, too. He bought him a 1967 Camaro with a 427 engine. Billy had all the extras put on that engine, too. And he topped it off with something I didn't have—namely, a 4.11 posi-traction rear axle.

People always said that car would be the death of me. But, ironically, it saved my life—along with my buddy Wes Armour—in the summer of 1984. A fellow tried to end an argument using a 12-gauge shotgun in the parking lot of Burger King. We left the guy standing, literally, in a cloud of tire smoke. His Jeep wasn't going to catch up with that GTO.

A few years later, cancer—under the vinyl top, in the trunk, and behind the wheel wells—would claim that old GTO. We would take the Holly and the Edelbrock and bolt it on top of the 400 engine in our mint condition 1973 Grand Am.

But things were never the same. In 1971, Congress put a halt to the golden era of great muscle cars in America. Emissions requirements would flood the market with low compression, two-barrel, single-exhaust versions of the old cars we used to love. They were merely shadows of their former selves. Our memories of the glory days, like so many youthful dreams, are fading in the rear-view mirror.

And what did Dad buy me when I turned sixteen, five years before Mike would reach that age? Nothing. Worse, he would not even let me buy a car with my own hard-earned money until I was in college—and even then, he only allowed me to buy a Ford Pinto! No, I'm not making this up, and yes, I resented it when,

just two years later, Mike was handed a cool muscle car—while my friends were laughing at me…

Eventually, however, I gained a different perspective. I'm glad that Mike got that car. Obviously, he treasured it, and now we have these stories.

Dad was wise to find an activity that he could do with Mike during his turbulent teenage years; otherwise, his life may not have turned out as well. I think one of the unstated morals to this story is that parents need to find ways to stay connected and relate to their kids.

When Mike passed, he left me his car: a beautiful 2019 Accord that he had purchased just the previous summer. It's the nicest car I have ever had—and I treasure it. Thank you, Mike. I'd much rather have you than your car, but I am grateful for what I do have.

My old car was still in excellent condition, so I gave it to a single mother from our church who had no car. Why? Because when Mike bought his new car in 2019, his old car was still in great shape, but he didn't trade it in; he gave it to a student who needed a car. That's the kind of guy he was. And that's how we change the world for the better—we set a good example for others to follow.

(Later, in the "Remembrances" chapter, Scott Maxson writes about "The Impact of Mike and the 1970 GTO.")

Mike: Upper left corner (dark jersey).

Picture of Ph.D. diploma.

CHAPTER 3

What Hard Work Does to Tragedy

Originally published in 2007 as "Life and How to Live It, Part IX."

If you didn't know Mike's past, you could easily assume that he was always studious and always made good grades. Quite the contrary—this was one of his dramatic transformations. But it wasn't quick or easy...

It's no secret that I wasn't the best student ever to attend Clear Lake High School. I failed English all four years. I failed to reach the 2.0 GPA mark. I finished in the bottom 1 percent of my graduating class. There was a distinct reason why I performed so poorly: I attempted to get a "D" in every class and to fail English every year so I did not have to get a summer job. The fact that I got above a 1.0 GPA was due to a bunch of accidental grades of "C" from some overly generous teachers.

My total lack of effort in high school was largely due to my success on the soccer field. At the age of fifteen, I won a state soccer championship together with some magnificently talented players—most notably, Joey Gunderson, Sam

Hinson, and Peter Royster. After Mike Olmedo and Steve Zobel joined our team, we would soon be headed for another state championship game. This time we were heavy favorites, with several players who had won a state title previously as underdogs. I was certain that I was one of several players on the team who were headed for the pros. In fact, I thought I was a lock.

But then something strange started happening at the end of my junior year. In April, I was averaging about sixty miles a week on the jogging trail as I was gearing up for a crack at the Houston marathon. As I was training, I began to hear and feel a small clicking noise around my left ankle. Over the next few months, it began to actually hurt so I went to see a doctor. The news wasn't good. A bone spur was starting to slice my Achilles tendon which, according to the doctor, would surely rupture without corrective surgery.

So, I did what you would expect me to do. I told the doctor to kiss my (backside) and kept on running through the injury. Needless to say, I eventually had to stop running completely. I was so hopelessly out of shape at the beginning of the next season that I could not even make the team.

I finally had the surgery in November. And it was unsuccessful. In fact, I would be unable to run even a single mile for over three years. Needless to say, my dream (the only one I ever had) of becoming a professional soccer player was over. I started smoking, drinking, and occasionally using drugs in preparation for a two-year sentence to junior college. There wasn't a university in America pathetic enough to take me. Not even Ole Miss. [*That's an inside joke—"Ole Miss" (the University of Mississippi) is the savage rival of Mississippi State University, which was Mike's and our father's alma mater.*]

But, nonetheless, I had to take the fall from being a star athlete at a great high school to an absolute nobody at a junior college in the pathetic little town of Pasadena, TX [*another rivalry, by the way*]. It was either that or work as a mechanic. Having rebuilt the engine on my 1970 GTO (together with my father) I could have gotten employment as a grease monkey somewhere in the Clear Lake area. But that was even worse than junior college in Pasadena. Needless to say, I was one miserable and angry eighteen-year-old.

Miserable as I was, I buckled down and after two years of misery, I was in a position to get into a four-year university. I applied and was accepted to Mississippi State University. It wasn't prestigious, but at least it wasn't Ole Miss. And my dad was so happy that I had started to turn things around that he rewarded me with an invitation to join a fraternity at his expense.

After I was initiated into the Sigma Chi fraternity, I did something very rare among Southeastern Conference Greeks: I managed to actually raise my GPA in my first full semester living in the fraternity house. In fact, it was now nearly double my high school GPA. Through a little perseverance, the GPA continued to climb despite my dwelling place in Room 13 of the Sigma Chi House. I was easily accepted to graduate school and started working on my M.S. degree right after finishing my B.A.

At the end of my M.S. program, I turned down an offer to pursue a doctorate in psychology at the University of Georgia. Instead, I finished my four-year doctoral program in just three years at Mississippi State. It wasn't the most prestigious place to get a Ph.D., but at least it wasn't Ole Miss.

I spent the week of graduation—my last week at Mississippi State—driving my friend Jerry's old Jeep Wrangler. He was borrowing my truck to move his things back to Vicksburg. Every night that week, I would go out driving my friends Dana, Stephanie, and Becky around town while they drank beer, and I enjoyed the company of three very pretty former members of the Phi Mu sorority—one of whom was also finishing grad school that week.

When Jerry got back in town, I offered to buy that old Jeep Wrangler from him. He laughed and said he would never sell the vehicle to a good friend. Jerry said it was so prone to breaking down that you would almost have to be a professional mechanic to keep it on the road.

At just that moment, I was struck with a profound realization: Had I not been unexpectedly injured, I would have been a former professional soccer player by then. And I would have been a professional mechanic without a single college degree by then, too. Instead, I was a twenty-eight-year-old Ph.D. who had just landed a good job in North Carolina.

There is no tragedy or setback so great that it cannot be turned into a blessing, with the help of a little persistence and hard work.

First, Mike was not against being a mechanic—if that is your calling. Obviously, it was not his, so it would have been the wrong choice for him. In fact, Mike once said to me something to the effect that we, as a nation, have made it too cheap and easy to attend college and pushed kids into college who weren't really interested and qualified to be there. This caused the student loan bubble and a general degradation of the college experience.

Second, I tried to convince Mike that the setback of his early retirement could well be a blessing in disguise. I reminded him that the three greatest tragedies of my life—being laid off unexpectedly the week before Christmas in 1996, my bitter divorce in 2005, and my near-fatal motorcycle accident in

2010—all turned out for the best, in time. I also reminded him that, just a few years ago, someone else close to us was also devastated by an unexpected early retirement—and that turned out to be a good thing after all.

As hard as I tried, I failed in my attempt to assure Mike that things would work out for the best. At the time, I sensed that maybe he was just politely letting me talk and that I wasn't really getting through to him. But I wasn't too worried about that, as I thought we would continue to have those talks over the coming months. I also hoped that the encouragement he was receiving from me and from his other close friends would ultimately help him to see that things weren't as bleak as he believed them to be. Unfortunately, I did not realize the actual depth of his discouragement until after the fact.

When discouraged by a tragedy or setback, please remember this story—and don't give up!

Ph.D. graduation, 1993.

We put a camper top on this truck and drove it to LA a few times Memorable road trips!

Mike in his office at UNCW, early in his career.

CHAPTER 4

A Good Father

Originally published in 2017, shortly after our father passed.

The previous chapter told the inspiring story of Mike's academic transformation. However, because his columns were constrained by size limitations, Mike lacked the space to explain Dad's major role as the architect of that transformation, so he had to make that a separate column. And I wanted to include it here, not just to flesh out the story and honor our father but because (as usual) Mike wrote the story to share the lessons he'd learned from these life experiences.

Occasionally, people ask me how a guy could go from having a 1.8 GPA in high school (and graduating 734th out of 740) to becoming a college professor.

My failure as a high school student was mostly due to my belief that I was such a good soccer player that I could simply skip college and go straight to the pros. That was fueled by a couple of coaches who tickled my ears with exaggerated assessments of my ability. But I should have known better. In retrospect, my goals (no pun intended) were out of proportion with my ability.

At the start of my senior year, I suffered a serious injury to my Achilles tendon. I tried to play through it but was unable to make the team. I had to undergo surgery. It took years to recover. My athletic career was finished.

I somehow managed to stumble through my senior year and graduate. When I finally did, my father gave me a gift I did not deserve. It was an expensive twelve-string guitar. I was such a bad student that I didn't even deserve a gift certificate to K-Mart. The guitar was undeserved, but I accepted it with deep gratitude.

My dad also gave me another gift for graduation. It was the gift of a second chance in school. Given my grades, there was not a university in America that would accept me. But Texas had a law that said junior colleges had to accept high school graduates, regardless of their grades. So, my dad graciously allowed me to live at home and attend the local junior college [San Jacinto]. But there was one condition: I could only take ten hours and I could not hold a full-time job. Dad wanted me to take it slow and get back on my feet again, academically speaking.

Dad's "take it slow" approach worked. At the end of the first semester, I had completed ten hours with a 2.7 GPA. It wasn't great, but it was an improvement. Dad complimented me on the improvement and urged me to increase my load to twelve hours during the spring semester.

At the end of my second semester, I had lifted my GPA to 2.9 with twelve more completed hours. Dad again complimented me on my improvement and urged me to increase my load to fifteen hours when I returned for my second year.

At the end of that crucial third semester, which was my first with a full five-course load, I had lifted my GPA to 3.0 with fifteen more completed hours. Dad again complimented me on my improvement and urged me to increase my load to eighteen hours.

At the end of my fourth semester, there was more success and steady improvement. I had lifted my GPA to 3.1 with eighteen completed hours. Dad again complimented me on my improvement. He also reminded me I was only seven hours away from an associate degree. He then did some homework and found that if I transferred to his alma mater, Mississippi State University, I could transfer hours back to San Jacinto to finish the two-year degree. Furthermore, as the son of an alumnus, I could get an out-of-state tuition waiver, which would save us enough money to allow me to join a fraternity. There was no way I was turning down that deal.

After I went off to Mississippi State, went through rush, pledged Sigma Chi, and moved into the fraternity house, something strange happened. My GPA shot all the way up to 3.4. In fact, I was probably the first man in the history of American higher education to raise his GPA while living in a fraternity house. Okay, that might be a slight exaggeration. But my grades were high enough for me to enter graduate school.

When I approached my dad about going to grad school, he was enthusiastic. In fact, he told me that since I had lived at home for two years and saved him so much money, he would be glad to help me out financially. I took him up on the offer and finished the master's program with a 3.9 GPA. By that point, I had decided to pursue a Ph.D. and become a college professor. That meant at least three more years of school.

When I told my dad I wanted to get my doctorate, his response was memorable: "Good luck with that, son. Your mom and I are broke. You're on your own!" But actually, I wasn't on my own. I had been practicing on that guitar that Dad gave me for high school graduation. In fact, after six long years of practice, I was good enough to earn a living playing music. So, I called my friend Shannon Ruscoe with a business idea. He was a very talented singer who was also struggling to make a living in grad school at Mississippi State. Together, we formed a musical duo, which helped me pay for my Ph.D. while Shannon studied engineering.

I eventually graduated in 1993, without a penny of debt. The undeserved gift my father had given me had been worth the expense. It generated enough money to take me all the way home on my long academic journey.

Whenever I tell people the story of how I went from the bottom of my class to being a college professor, they immediately recognize the hero of the story. It isn't me. It's my father.

What Mike wrote about Dad is touching and instructive. But what Mike chose not to write is also very instructive. You see, our father was a human being, which means that he was not perfect. And yet Mike chose to focus instead on Dad's strengths and contributions because he understood that those are what actually count as important.

I used to do the opposite, complaining about Dad's imperfections. Later in life, however, I followed Mike's good example and developed a deep appreciation for my father. That choice made me a better person. This goes to show that the fifth commandment is not just for the benefit of parents.

Mike once said, "Commandments are ultimately things we are told to do because we're too dense to know that they're really for our own good." *Yes, indeed.*

Shannon and Mike, J. C. Garcia's, Starkville, MS, February 1990.

Anne and Mike, Mississippi State University, October 1991.

CHAPTER 5

Shannon and Mike and Anne

Originally published in 2012 as "How Obama Earned My Doctorate."

In the previous chapter, Mike briefly mentioned that Dad gave him a guitar in high school and that he was able to use it to work his way through grad school. I always admired his musical talent and his work ethic, so I'm glad he wrote a column specifically about that experience and what he learned from it.

Back in 1989, I decided to pursue a Ph.D. in Criminology. I was nearing the end of my master's program in Psychology. I had a teaching assistantship that paid a mere $345 per month. I knew that I could not live on $345 per month for the minimum of three years I would need to finish my doctorate. I also knew that my parents would not be able to extend the same financial support they had so graciously extended while I was working in my master's degree. So, I devised a plan to start a new business with just a $1,000 initial investment.

My grandfather had passed away in December of 1988. In the late spring of 1989, my grandmother mailed me a check for $1,000 that had been part of a life insurance policy payout issued upon my grandfather's death. In the late summer of 1989, I met a graduate student by the name of Shannon Ruscoe. He had been playing tennis with my roommate, Harry Wilson, the day I met him. I was sitting in my living room playing a song by James Taylor when Shannon started singing along. After just a few minutes of listening to Shannon sing, I knew my life would never be the same again.

I called Shannon later that fall and asked if he wanted to get together and rehearse a few songs. We did. Within a few weeks we were hanging out at keg parties in places like Starkville's College Station apartment complex. After a few beers, I would go to my car and get my 12-string. As our repertoire increased, so did Shannon's confidence as a singer.

After a few months of getting to know Shannon, I laid out a plan. I found a beautiful Alvarez six-string with a cedar top and black jacaranda back and sides. I realized I could buy the guitar and install a Martin thin-line pickup under the bridge for just $700. With the remaining $300, I told Shannon that, for just $30 per night, we could rent a PA system from our friend Jim Beaty, the owner of Backstage Music in Starkville. The idea was that after playing free ten times we could start to earn a living as musicians.

First, we had to find a place to play. Fortunately, a Kappa Sigma named Mike worked as a manager at J.C. Garcia's—a Mexican restaurant/bar that featured acoustic acts, including the legendary Jeff Cummings and Jeffrey Rupp. We went to see him with an offer, telling Mike we would play free of charge on a Tuesday night, but only on one condition: if they sold $2,000 worth of liquor, they would have to hire us the next week for 10 percent of the liquor sales, or $200.

Mike laughed. J.C.'s had never sold $2,000 worth of liquor on a Tuesday night, which was generally their slowest night of the week. Naturally, he felt he had nothing to lose. So, we booked our first gig at a real restaurant in a real college town.

I called all of my old friends at the Sigma Chi house and told them to show up at J.C.'s the following Tuesday night. Shannon told all the girls at the Chi Omega house where he worked as a "houseboy" in his spare time. As a result of our marketing, we packed the place out. J.C.'s sold over $2,000 in liquor that night, and we were invited to come back the next week.

Playing free at keg parties also paid off. By May of 1990, we were getting hired to play private parties. At one of those parties, we met the manager of the Bully III, a restaurant/bar near downtown Starkville. His name was David Lee Odom. He upped our salary to $250 per night, plus free dinner and free beer. By the time I graduated, I had played in that bar over one hundred times. It was there that I met other musicians and eventually had a chance to play all over the state and region. As a businessman and friend, Dave Odom changed our lives forever.

After Shannon moved to Nashville in 1991, I decided it was time to rely on the government for financial support. I'm just kidding. I simply went out and found another great singer named Anne Ford. We would play together until 1993. Our act was so successful that in April of 1993, my last full month of college, we had played a whopping twenty-two gigs in just thirty days.

As a result of my business venture, I was able to graduate with a Ph.D. without taking out a single student loan. And it *was* a business venture. I was not just a guitarist. I booked most of our gigs, handled equipment purchases, and did a modest bit of accounting.

The irony is that, back in those days, I was a Democrat with socialist leanings. I voted for Dukakis and Clinton as the "lesser of two evils"—all the while complaining about the lack of a far-left alternative. Shortly thereafter, I would get involved in a two-year relationship with the daughter of the head of the socialist party of Ecuador. I simply failed to reconcile the discrepancies between my theoretical view of the world and my real-world experiences. Eventually, I grew out of my childish socialist mindset and realized that capitalism had allowed me to utilize my God-given talents to earn a living that government could never provide.

I am grateful to have had the opportunity to visit Mike in school and watch him perform at several venues. Although he never played again professionally, Mike retained an abiding love of music. He had eight outstanding guitars when he passed.

While I was clearing out his house, I found original recordings of him playing with Shannon and Anne, along with pictures and flyers from that time, and I put together several slide show videos, which I shared on my YouTube account:

Fleetwood Mac's "Songbird" performed by Mike and Anne.

https://www.youtube.com/
watch?v=jqPrBB7Dg7Q&ab_channel=DaveAdams

Neil Young's "Heart of Gold" performed by Mike and Shannon.

https://www.youtube.com/
watch?v=aP5d1-NCA6I&ab_channel=DaveAdams

This chapter is also a foreshadowing of Mike's political transformation, and we will delve into that soon in Chapter 11.

Our mother, Marilyn,
and her mother, Nell.
New Orleans, 1937.

First picture of Mike with Mom.
Columbus, Mississippi, 1964.

Clear Lake (Houston), 1978.

CHAPTER 6

A Good Mother

Originally published in 2006 as "Life and How to Live It, Part V."

We've just read how Dad was the architect of Mike's academic and vocational transformation. So, where was Mom when this was going on? Right there beside them, of course. But her influence, albeit more subtle, was more profound, building a foundation for her son's future spiritual transformation. To understand why Mike was so principled, one must understand our mother, Marilyn Rester Adams.

Mom was heavily influenced by her mother, Nell Myers Rester, and her grandmother, Julia Lee Myers ("Big Mama"). Three generations of solid, humble, loving, Christian women. I cannot overstate the influence of these amazing women on their friends and families. The article below is one of my favorites.

Recently, a conservative atheist wrote a very angry yet moving letter about the passing of his wife. She suffered from cancer for a prolonged period of time. Apparently, she was in terrible pain for months before she finally passed. After decades of marriage, he found himself alone in a house full of memories. That's when he wrote me, insisting there isn't a God and urging me to "get off of religion" and stick to my "bread-and-butter" topic of campus censorship.

The letter reminds me of another great woman who died of cancer. The year was 1962. The woman's name was Nell Myers Rester. She was my maternal grandmother.

Nell's death at the age of forty-eight was probably the result of an error by the physician who removed a cancerous organ during a prior surgery. Later, when another organ was consumed by cancer, the doctor was consumed by guilt. He concluded that he could have also removed the other organ and, thus, saved her life. After it was too late, he tearfully apologized to her at her bedside. That was back in the days when doctors spoke honestly to their patients instead of worrying about future litigation.

When my grandmother passed, that doctor drove from New Orleans to Gulfport to attend her funeral. There, he told my mother that for years he had to console patients, but that Nell Myers was the only patient he ever had who tried to console him. That story was corroborated by several black nurses who had asked to come along to Nell's funeral. That was rare in the segregated Mississippi of 1962.

The consensus was that Nell didn't care that the doctor probably made a mistake that prematurely ended her life. She only wanted to make sure that he was all right and that he knew he was forgiven. During the advanced stages of her illness, she even wrote him an uplifting letter that he kept in his office desk for the rest of his career.

And the doctor wasn't the only one changed forever by the way my grandmother handled her bout with cancer. My mother—upon hearing the doctor's tearful account of Nell's loving treatment of him—decided that her faith in the face of adversity was conclusive proof of the power of an Almighty.

So, she set about proving an important point regarding life and how to live it:

Whether a tragedy remains a tragedy or becomes a catalyst for good is entirely a function of individual free will.

And so, my mother was soon collecting money door-to-door for the American Cancer Society. When I was a young boy, I remember cigarette smokers slamming the door in her face. But she just kept on going for years after her mother's death.

And then there were the trips to the worst slums in Houston. Mom would buy a bag of groceries and just knock on someone's door in the ghetto to deliver them unannounced. I remember the way the recipient's face would light up when she just walked away without asking for anything in return. She didn't even need to open her mouth to witness to them.

Then there were the prisoners she began writing to in the 1970s. I never saw their faces until twenty years later when I began visiting prisoners myself. That was when I was thirty-two—about thirty-four years after Nell died. About that time, I realized I really had known my maternal grandmother after all.

Of course, it doesn't take a tragic death to transform a life from one of complacency to one of great works. In fact, it is a dual tragedy when we wait for a tragedy to take hold of our lives and force us to choose a life of gratitude over a life of self-pity.

Rather than praying to God the same way you talk to your store-bound spouse—merely listing the things you want Him to get you—you should confine yourself to enumerating the blessings you already have. In fact, you could do it in alphabetical order—picking one blessing for every letter. If you follow my advice, your only problem will be choosing

41

between the many blessings you have but rarely even think about.

And that proves another point about life and how to live it:

Self-pity and gratitude are mortal enemies. Where one exists, the other cannot.

There was not enough space for the above article to make it clear that Mom was very different when she was young and that her mother's death didn't just inspire her to do good works. It transformed her—and for the better. Mike would explain this very eloquently in his powerful eulogy at Mom's memorial service in 2019. Here is an excerpt:

There is a real misconception about my mother. People believe that she was always a devout committed Christian throughout her entire life, and that is not true. When she got out of high school and through the college years and early adulthood, she was what you would call a nominal Christian. She just identified as a Christian, but really didn't live that life.

In 1961, her mother, Nell Myers Rester, became ill with cancer. In 1962, she passed away. It was a transformational moment in my mother's life. At that funeral, my mother really came to three realizations.

The first thing she thought was, "My mother is irreplaceable. There's no possible way she could be replaced."

But the second thing she realized was that there was a great deficiency in her life at that point. She saw a contrast between the way she was living and the way that Nell had been living.

And then there was this third realization that she just needed to try. She needed to make an effort to try and close that gap between her life and the witness that her mother had been living.

And so, my mother began to do just that. She started with daily Bible study and prayer for about five years after Nell's death, and she became more committed to Christianity.

[*Mike continues to talk about the many things Mom had done, including things he mentioned in the above article, before concluding with this*:]

My mother won big battles. Like the battle over my spiritual destiny, and over my father's, and there were so many big battles that she fought faithfully day in [and] day out for years, and she won. Now, I don't want people to walk out of here today and think, well, to be a great person you have to do great things. Pick big battles and win big battles. That's not true.

Because the greatness of my mother was in her day-to-day interactions with people.

As individuals, we may have doctrinal differences. But I will tell you this: if there's one thing that we know about God with absolute certainty, it is that He cares very much about how human beings treat one another. And my mother was deeply invested in every single person that she ever encountered.

And what she would want is for today to be a very positive day, a very positive experience. And I'm convinced that three things need to happen here today:

First, we need to acknowledge that we do feel that my mother was irreplaceable. I mean, let's face it. There are so many people in this room who are thinking that right now: there will never be another Marilyn Adams.

But it's also very important that at least one of us comes to a realization. There's something missing in our life; there's something deficient in our life, and I know that's going to be fulfilled today.

Because I know that's the way I feel when I look back at my mother's life, and then I look at my own. I say there's a deficiency there.

But then a third thing needs to happen. And that's the third thing that happened at her own mother's funeral when she decided that it was time for her, even though she thought her mother was irreplaceable, to make an effort to do so anyway. To begin to walk with God daily. And to honestly endeavor because, really, there are only two different possibilities out there. You could be successful. You could try to be like my mother and live that kind of life and you could succeed. My mother succeeded in becoming the kind of mother that her own mother was. The good news is that if we put in an honest effort to do that, and we fail, we still will have impacted the lives of many people in a very positive way.

I think what Mother wanted for today is for us to acknowledge the reality that death, within the Christian worldview, is an opportunity for rebirth and for rejuvenation. That is the way it was for her. And the fact of the matter is that the idea of rebirth and rejuvenation through death is actually the entire story of Christianity.

I feel the same way about Mom that Mike does—that there is a deficiency between Mom and myself—but I also see a deficiency between Mike and myself, and I want to narrow those gaps. I know Mike wants us to see his loss—and every loss—as an opportunity for rebirth and for rejuvenation.

Photo by Mike of the Virgin of El Panecillo, also known as the Virgin of Quito, in Quito, Ecuador.

CHAPTER 7

The Shadow Proves the Sunshine

*Originally published in 2008. The title is also the title of a song
by Switchfoot, one of Mike's favorite bands.*

*Mike's 1996 trip to Ecuador was a major life experience for him;
it was key to his spiritual transformation, to his turning away
from his avowed atheism. Mike often spoke of this in his speeches
and writings, as he does below.*

This morning I received an email that was so touching and
so important I had to respond with a full column rather than
a short email. Actually, I could write a number of columns in
response to the email. But, for now, I'll just respond to these
two important lines imbedded in its first paragraph: "Right
now I'm in doubt about the existence of a God at all. I'd
like to know more about what you believe—how you look at
tragedy and evil in relation to a loving God."

What the reader is asking, in effect, is how can one
believe in God despite the existence of evil. In my case,
abandoning atheism came about because of the existence of
evil and a desire to see justice in its aftermath.

The very second the inner gates of that Ecuadorian prison opened up, I could smell the foul odor of rotten food, urine, and solid waste. I knew, to the very core of my being, that it was wrong of the government to have no maintenance budget for that 150-year-old prison. It was wrong to let prisoners walk around through puddles of their own urine mixed with fecal matter as they awaited trial for years—even for offenses carrying sentences of mere months.

When Pedro told me he had been acquitted weeks before but was still in prison, I again smelled something rotten. I knew it was pure evil that led the officials to force him to raise money for "processing fees" in order to set him free after four years of wrongful incarceration.

As I walked into the thirty-six-square-meter cell, I saw forty-five men staring back at me—some of them wearing the same rotting clothes they wore the day they were arrested months or years before. When I saw a butcher knife sitting on top of a broken TV set, I knew why so many of the prisoners wore bandages. And I knew it was pure evil that kept the guards from seizing the weapons and from even caring that prisoners killed other prisoners every day.

When I saw a young man—he appeared to be a teenager—up against a wall being beaten with a club, I knew that I was witnessing pure evil. The guards quickly stopped the beating because they knew it, too. As I heard the sound of that club whacking against his torso, I wasn't sure whether I heard the sound of bones breaking. But I knew I was witnessing evil.

It was that same sick feeling I had when I first went to the Holocaust Museum in Washington, D.C. The pictures of those bodies piled upon bodies at Auschwitz made me sick to my stomach immediately. No one had to teach me to feel sick. I just did. It was because of what God had written on my heart.

And I felt very sick again when I walked into that prison kitchen and peered down into the boiling vats. I asked the cook to explain why they were boiling everything - the fruit, the vegetables, and the meat. It was because it had all started to rot after no one would buy it in the old town market in Quito. So, they sold it to the prison officials who tried to boil off the rot before serving it to the prisoners.

As I walked out of the prison doors, I thought of the guards telling me they did not need capital punishment. When they wanted to shoot someone, they just told them they were free to go, shot them in the back, and reported it as an attempted escape.

But no one was shooting at me as I looked up at the statue of the Virgin Mary. [*Mike had the presence of mind to take a picture of it, and that is the picture at the beginning of this chapter.*] I was free to walk out of the prison and out of the shadows of evil and darkness that shook me to the core on that damp March afternoon.

It was at that very moment that I recognized the wrongfulness of my hardened atheism. I knew then that those dark shadows were conclusive proof of the existence of the sunshine. Without the sun, I would not know what darkness was. And without the Son, I could not escape it.

The reader who inspired this column asked how I look at tragedy and evil in relation to a loving God. That is simple: I look at tragedy and evil in relation to a loving God.

Mike's death was a tragedy, and the way he was treated was evil.

You don't have to go to a foreign land to get closer to God; it can happen anywhere, at the most unexpected times. In fact, in the next chapter, for Mike's next epiphany, we go to Huntsville, Texas. That's where my parents ended up after they retired early from their NASA careers and bought a nice little house on nine acres in the country. The young couple who had built the house were getting divorced—and, thankfully, they threw in their young yellow lab with the house. Jake ended up being our favorite dog ever.

Mother once told me that those were the best years of her life, in that house in her sixties. Dad was happy there too, but he did feel that he was too young and too poor to not still be working. Fortunately, the Texas prison system in Huntsville was looking for an IT guy with his qualifications. Since Mike just happened to be a professor of criminal justice, this was, as you shall see, Divine Providence at work...

STATE OF TEXAS
OFFICE OF THE GOVERNOR

GEORGE W. BUSH
GOVERNOR

August 24, 2000

Mike S. Adams, Ph.D.
Associate Professor of Criminal Justice
The University of North Carolina at Wilmington
601 South College Road
Wilmington, NC 28403

Dear Dr. Adams:

Thank you for a copy of your recent column about capital punishment in Texas.
Although you and I differ in our beliefs about the death penalty, I appreciate receiving
your strong and eloquent viewpoint.

Best wishes.

Sincerely,

GEORGE W. BUSH

GWB:smg

*Mike wrote several articles about death-row inmate
Johnny Paul Penry (see below), which elicited this
response from then Governor George W. Bush.*

CHAPTER 8

Everlasting Life on Death Row

Originally published in early 2020.

Mike's trip to Ecuador broke atheism's hold on him, but it did not lead him all the way back to Christianity. To complete his spiritual transformation, Mike needed to make another prison visit—this time, in Texas...

Every time I get the chance, I use my extended break between semesters to take a road trip through Mississippi, where I was born, and then back to Texas, where I grew up. Visiting friends and family and seeing my old childhood homes gives me a chance to think about where I am going by reflecting on where I have been. This year's road trip just happened to conclude on December 30th, which was the twentieth anniversary of an important milestone in a larger personal journey. It was the day I interviewed Johnny Paul Penry on Texas death row, just a few miles from my parents' house, and just thirteen days before his scheduled execution.

Johnny Paul Penry was a vicious rapist and killer. His first rape put him in prison, but he was paroled after just two years. While on parole, he committed his second rape, which concluded with his murder of the young victim. He beat her so badly that he burst both of her kidneys. He then finished her off by shoving a pair of scissors into her heart. When he was later convicted and sentenced to die, his lawyers argued that he was mentally retarded [*today termed "intellectually disabled"*] and thus should not be executed per the Eighth Amendment ban on Cruel and Unusual Punishment.

After Penry's case had wound its way through the justice system for twenty years, which included two trips to the Supreme Court, his execution date was reset for the third and what appeared to be final time. My dad had taken a retirement job in the very building where Texas executions took place. Furthermore, our neighbor happened to be the warden. Thus, when I expressed interest in interviewing Penry prior to his scheduled execution, it was not hard for me to make the arrangements.

My goal was pretty simple when I arrived on death row on that second-to-last morning of the twentieth century. I simply wanted to gather important information so I could do a better job of teaching the case to my students. I had been teaching the *Penry v. Lynaugh* ruling (issued by the Supreme Court in 1989) for several years, because it addressed some important constitutional and philosophical questions. I had no idea that the interview would affect me so personally.

As I spoke with Penry, we broached the topic of his alleged history of abuse at the hands of his mother. During that portion of the interview, I was convinced of two things. One was that some of his claims were valid. The other was that some of his claims had been manufactured in order to win sympathy in the court of public opinion, as well as leniency in a court of law.

Similarly, as we broached the topic of his claims of mental retardation, I was also convinced of two things. One was that there was objective evidence, gathered prior to his criminal career, which demonstrated a clear pattern of at least mild mental retardation. The other was that his claims of mental deficiency had been exaggerated in order to win sympathy in the court of public opinion, as well as leniency in a court of law.

After I had gathered all of the information I was seeking, I stood up and placed my hand on the glass in order to do the so-called death row handshake with Penry—just as he placed his hand on the other side of the glass. That was the moment that something surreal happened. Shortly after telling me he was scared of being executed, he recited John 3:16 to me, to the best of his limited cognitive ability.

Naturally, I had to ask Penry whether he had actually read the Bible. He indicated that after learning how to read and write on death row, he had read the entire Bible over the course of his many years as a condemned man. After he told me that, I turned and walked away. As I left the prison, I concluded that Penry had read the Bible out of sheer boredom over the course of two decades. But there were clear reasons to doubt that he had any kind of legitimate conversion experience. *BASED ON WHOSE OPINION?*

As I made the drive back to my parents' house, I was overwhelmed by the emotion of the day. Simply imagining a brutal rape or murder is overwhelming. But the details of Penry's miserable life struck to the core of me, as well. To compound things, there is just something sobering about being on death row. Even my dog knew I was upset when I got home. He followed me around and kept sticking his head under my hand to remind me that petting him would put me at ease.

But it was difficult for me to feel at ease knowing that a convicted murderer and rapist with substantial mental limitations had read the Bible, while I had not. After all, I was already a tenured professor. How could I call myself educated, having not read the most important book ever put in print? That question led me to make one of the most important decisions I ever made in my life. I was going to go home, buy a copy of the Bible, and read it from cover to cover in the coming year.

I took six breaks and read six apologetic books as I worked my way through the King James Version. [*Elsewhere, Mike added:* "It took an additional two years to read four more translations of the Bible (the NRSV, GNT, NIV, and NASB)." *Mike was always thorough!*] When I finished, I became the only conservative Christian in a department full of tenured Marxists. Although the transformation led to a lot of conflict and eventually seven years of litigation in federal court, it was certainly worth it. I had gone there on a mission to help save Johnny Paul Penry from death row. But I ended up being the one who had his death sentence commuted.

This story is for those who consider their own past sins to be an irreversible judgment of death. I have told it before but tell it again because I want people to consider the implications of the fact that God can use even a mentally retarded rapist and murderer for a larger kingdom purpose.

To state the rather obvious point of the column, if Johnny Paul Penry can be used by God, then so can you. So please, don't wallow in self-pity. Know that you are still valuable. And that you are still needed in doing the difficult work of reaching lost souls wherever you may find them.

Mike didn't say which six books he read, but elsewhere, he wrote that these were his favorites:

1. *How Now Shall We Live* by Charles Colson and Nancy Pearcey. This may be the best book (besides the Bible) that I have ever read. One can use this book to begin applying what one learns in the Bible to important contemporary issues. The "recommended readings" section at the end is worth the price of the book.

2. *Mere Christianity* by C.S. Lewis. When I was younger, I held many ridiculous beliefs. Among them was the notion that Jesus was a great moral teacher, though not divine. That is simply absurd. Jesus claimed to be God. If he wasn't, then he was a liar, which would disqualify Him from being a great moral teacher. Reading Lewis helped me get past such nonsense. This book also provides a strong argument for the existence of an absolute moral code. Reading this book convinced me that most self-proclaimed atheists really aren't atheists. They believe in God and are angry at Him because they think He is unjust.

3. *Christian Apologetics* by Norm Geisler. I thought this was a great apologetic when I read it ten years ago. But some may want to go with the more recent *I Don't Have Enough Faith to be an Atheist*, which Geisler co-wrote with my good friend Frank Turek. The latter selection has a special place in my heart since a friend of mine read it thrice and converted to Christianity while he was dying (and did not yet know he was dying).

4. *Scaling the Secular City* by J.P. Moreland. I read this book in just a couple of days and loved every page of it. Since then, I have met J.P. and have heard him lecture several times. On the basis of those lectures, I decided to read another of his books called *Love God with All Your Mind*. I liked it even more.

Coincidentally, at the same time that Mike was making his way back to God, I was having a spiritual journey of my own. When I left home, I left my church and my God behind. I did not actually become an atheist, as Mike did, but I had the false belief that I could live my own way just fine without God. It took me over two decades to finally admit I was wrong. I was visiting Mike in 2001, and I told him I was having second thoughts about my decision to live without God. He knew just what I needed and took me to Barnes & Noble, where he told me to buy Mere Christianity. *I started reading it on the airplane on the way home, and it deeply resonated with me. Shortly thereafter, I went back to church. Mike did not preach to me, but he was prepared when I was ready—what a great lesson that is!*

CHAPTER 9

Life Chose Me

Mike would grow to become a strong and effective advocate for the unborn; in fact, that cause was one of his greatest passions. You can read more about this in his posthumously published book, Aborting Free Speech. *However, as Mike used to be pro-abortion, how did this transformation occur? Although he has told this story often, I think it is best told in the following article, written in 2012:*

In the summer of 1993, I went home for my ten-year high school reunion. I was so excited, I could hardly sleep all week. The kid who finished 734th in a class of 740 had made quite a turn-around. Over a span of ten years, I had gone off to junior college and earned an associate degree in Psychology. Next, I added a bachelor's degree in Psychology. Then, I earned a master's in Social Psychology. Finally, I topped it off with a doctorate in Criminology. I could hardly wait to see my old classmates and tell them that I had just been hired as a college professor. I could not wait to see their reaction as I told them that the guy who failed English four times in high school was now a published author. But those were not the only changes that had taken place over the course of ten years. I had also become an atheist and a strong proponent of abortion.

With all of that education, I should have known better. When my professors told me the object of abortion was "nothing more than a clump of cells," I should have known that there was a powerful incentive for me to believe them. I should have known there was a psychological motive to avoid examining all of the evidence in the debate. If psychology had taught me anything, it taught me that attitudes and beliefs do not always drive our behavior. Often, it is our behavior that drives our attitudes and beliefs.

My behavior in those days was reprehensible. But it did not become that way overnight. It was all part of a gradual decline that began during my senior year in high school. A torn Achilles tendon ended my dreams of becoming a professional soccer player. And that's when I started to smoke and drink heavily and run around with women whose affections assuaged my damaged self-esteem.

By the end of my first semester in junior college, I was calling myself an agnostic. And that helped accelerate the decline in my quality of life. As an undergraduate, I gradually increased my consumption of alcohol and my casual relationships with women. In 1989, I joined a musical duo. As a traveling musician, I further increased my consumption of alcohol. I not only abused alcohol but also used the women I met at the bars in which I played. It is true that many women who follow musicians are looking for the same thing. But that isn't true of all of them. I usually kept a steady girlfriend as well as a couple of extra women on the side. And because I did not behave responsibly with them, I needed a backup plan. That's how I came to convince myself that abortion was permissible. My beliefs about abortion had nothing to do with moral reasoning. It was all about rationalizing a lifestyle. It was about finding a way, psychologically speaking, of dealing with unpleasant thoughts about the risks I was taking.

I'm convinced that others were like me—they began studying psychology because of a desire to solve their own problems, not because they wanted to help other people. I learned about a lot of theories as a student of psychology, but I always seemed to lack the objectivity necessary to apply them to my own conduct.

Cognitive dissonance is a psychological theory, which asserts that human beings desire consistency in their cognitive life. In other words, it teaches that our beliefs and values and awareness of our behavior must all mesh with one another. When we feel tension between inconsistent beliefs and values, we sometimes adopt a new belief to resolve that tension. As a student of psychology, I was a living example of that theory without even realizing it.

AND THE CLAP!

I knew that sleeping with numerous women created a real risk of an unplanned pregnancy. I also knew that as a musician/student I was in no position to raise a child. But I was also raised to believe that abortion was wrong. So, I experienced real tension between my values and the awareness of my risky behavior and the consequences it might bring. I took the easy way out: I adopted the bland assertions of pro-choice advocates who claimed that the unborn were not human.

The behavior drove the attitudes. That is how the vicious cycle began. Once I had convinced myself that abortion was permissible because the unborn were not human, I sought out women who believed the same thing. In 1990, I went to the extreme of actually breaking up with a girlfriend as soon as she told me she would never have an abortion. Over the course of the next several years, I only dated women who were pro-choice. In other words, I would only date a woman if she was committed to giving me sex without the prospect of parenthood.

But all of that began to change in 1993 when I came home for that ten-year high school reunion. By God's Divine Providence, there were a couple of guests staying at my parents' house in Houston. Their names were Steve and Lisa Chambers. They were old friends we had met in 1969 when my mother was doing visitation for Clear Lake Baptist Church. *[And they would remain among our closest lifelong friends.]*

After I became an atheist and a liberal, Lisa Chambers refused to give up on me. Every time she would see me, she would try to plant a stone in my shoe in the hopes that I would re-think at least one of my political or religious positions. In 1993, when I sat down to eat breakfast with her at my parents' house, she decided to whittle away at my pro-choice position. After I admitted that I was pro-choice, she began telling me about a friend of one of her sons who had worked at a pregnancy center. That was when I first heard about the effects of ultrasound technology on a woman's likelihood of going through with an abortion.

After telling me a little bit about ultrasound technology, Lisa talked about a man named Bernard Nathanson, the co-founder of the National Abortion Rights Action League, or NARAL. She explained that Dr. Nathanson had performed hundreds of abortions, including one on his girlfriend. But after aborting his own child, Dr. Nathanson would eventually see an ultrasound of an actual abortion procedure. And it would change his life forever.

Bernard Nathanson would later convert to Roman Catholicism and join the pro-life movement. He also made a film called *The Silent Scream* (1984), which featured an ultrasound of an actual abortion as it was taking place. Lisa Chambers saw that film and recommended that I watch it, too. She also took the time to describe to me the ultrasound image of the child as it attempted to escape from the medical instrument that was dismembering it methodically. She also described the image of the baby's mouth opening and trying to scream—although no one could hear it from within the mother's womb. Lisa spent no more than a few minutes describing that imagery, but I could not seem to get it out of my mind.

So, I eventually watched *The Silent Scream*. And I also listened to what critics said about the movie. I was unimpressed with virtually all of what the critics had to say. The only rebuttal I ever heard in response to the movie's central claim—that the unborn actually felt the pain of abortion—was the so-called "reflex" argument. This was simply the claim that the baby was not recoiling in pain as a result of being dismembered by the surgeon's knife. Instead, it was argued that the baby was simply reacting reflexively from being touched by an unknown object. But the argument fails for one simple reason: if it has fully functioning reflexes, then the baby is a living being. It is not a mere blob of tissue.

Whether it was actively fighting or reflexively reacting, the thing I saw was surely living. And if it was a living being, then how could one escape the conclusion that it was a living human being? Surely, no one could assert that it was a member of another species until its birth.

The criminologist in me also had questions concerning the presumption of innocence: If there is any ambiguity about whether the unborn is human, then should it not be resolved in favor of calling it a human being? In the eyes of the law, is it not better to let ten guilty men go free than to wrongfully punish one innocent man? And if the human being has never committed a crime, then doesn't abortion always kill an innocent human being without due process?

While some have argued that the constitution includes an "implicit right to privacy," I saw nothing of the sort actually written into the United States Constitution. Instead, I saw specific mention of the "person" who is entitled to both "due process" and "equal protection." The words are there and need not be read into a "living" constitution—ironically, to justify killing.

Eventually, I concluded that it is up to the proponent of abortion to distinguish between an innocent human being and a "person." The burden rests upon those who wish to sentence the unborn to death. They must show "it" is not a person. For years, I've been asking pro-abortion-choicers to draw that distinction, and I've never been satisfied with their answers. Few have even tried to supply an answer based on science and reason. Ironically, since I've become a Christian, I have found that I do not need to rely on religion to make the case for life. Science and reason are enough. Of course, both, like life itself, are gifts from a God who is at once a lover of life and the author of truth.

When one examines my journey from abortion-choice advocate to pro-life activist, there is obvious cause for alarm. How could a man spend ten years in college, earn an M.S. in Psychology and a Ph.D. in Criminology, and never even think about the central question in the abortion debate? The fact that people were calling me "Dr." before I ever seriously answered the question "Are the unborn human?" is disturbing. It speaks volumes about the lack of intellectual diversity in higher education.

However, there is also good news: Notice that it all began with one person deciding to plant a stone in my shoe. Lisa Chambers did not set out to argue with me until I changed my mind. Had she done so, I would not have listened to her. My heart was not in the right place, and she knew it. Instead, she decided she would simply plant a stone in my shoe by spending about fifteen minutes with me and making sure that I began to think seriously about the central issue in the abortion debate: Are the unborn living human beings? That was all that was needed to create a great awakening in my conscience. I began to fundamentally rethink the issue of abortion.

Please remember this lesson and use it to your advantage. When someone you want to influence is simply not listening, go and find yourself a stone. Slip it into their shoe so that every time they take a step, they will be reminded of it. Let their growing discomfort with their own position cause them to stop and re-evaluate their thinking. You don't have to beat them over the head. You just have to leverage their own weight—the weight of their inner conscience—against them.

As I write these closing words, I am 2,000 miles from home. In three hours, I will speak to 200 students here in Colorado. We'll talk about how to defend life using logic paired with basic scientific evidence. In a few weeks, I'll fly to Pennsylvania to do the same thing. A few weeks later, I'll travel to North Carolina to give that message again. After nineteen years, the stone Lisa Chambers planted in my shoe is still there. As I travel around the country, I still feel its presence with every step I take.

And travel around the country, he did, giving speeches and participating in debates. Mike's most illustrious debate—and one of his proudest accomplishments—was with abortion provider Dr. Willie Parker. He prepared meticulously for his debate.

To read a transcript of this debate and to read more of Mike's writings on abortion, please read his posthumously published book, Aborting Free Speech. *Mike also wrote persuasively about abortion in Chapters 8 through 11 of his 2013 book,* Letters to a Young Progressive. *I mention these resources to emphasize that this chapter alone does not do justice to Mike's passion for and contributions towards saving the lives of innocent, defenseless, unborn children.*

August 20, 1997

University of North Carolina School of Law
Chapel Hill, North Carolina 27599-3380

RE: Michael S. Adams

I am delighted to write a letter of support for Dr. Mike Adams who has applied for admission to your law school. I have known Dr. Adams since he came to this campus four years ago. I was his department chair and immediate supervisor during that time (I rotated out of the chair position last year). In short, I know him very well.

I realize that it is a routine matter for admission committees to read countless "glowing" letters of recommendation. In this case, however, I am writing a letter for a genuinely exceptional individual. In my estimation, he is not only ideally suited to study law but I would anticipate that he will embark on a distinguished law-related career. Allow me to elaborate.

I have been a university professor for nineteen years and I have served on and chaired dozens of faculty hiring committees. I can state unequivocally that Mike Adams is the best young professorial talent that I have seen in my career. Many of the skills that make him an outstanding faculty member are no doubt transferable to the study and practice of law.

First, Dr. Adams is a gifted teacher. He is an engaging and dynamic classroom teacher who is also knowledgeable, well-organized, thorough, and rigorous. He consistently receives *the* highest student ratings among the department's twenty eight faculty. Students flock to his classes and rave about his teaching frequently noting that he is the best professor they have had. Senior faculty who have observed him in the classroom, including myself, are equally impressed. What makes Dr. Adams so effective as a communicator and public speaker is that he combines style *and* substance. He has exceptional oratory skills but he also knows what he is talking about and he is able to convey this to his audience. These are demonstrated qualities and not just raw potential which I presume would have high transferability to the study and practice of law.

Second, Professor Adams is a well trained and productive scholar. He has excellent research skills and is both theoretically and methodologically sophisticated. His research is careful, methodical, and insightful. His written publications demonstrate both close attention to detail and coherence and consistency of argument in relating evidence to support his conclusions. These are demonstrated skills which, again, I assume would translate well to the study and practice of law. In addition, Dr. Adams' area of substantive expertise is criminology, which has direct connection to the criminal justice system. His particular line of research focuses on various aspects of juvenile delinquency and minorities and crime and is being regularly published in respected outlets. Indeed, it was Mike's interest in the legal aspects of the criminal justice system that has prompted his interest in pursing a law career.

Finally, Mike is a genuinely good colleague and university citizen. From a department chair's perspective, he is an especially valuable faculty resource who represents the department well in the media and in other public forums. Mike has an outgoing and personable manner and has ingratiated himself to faculty and students alike with his wit and good nature. He is also a knowledgeable and insightful sociologist who adds a great deal to the intellectual lifeblood of this department.

Despite my best efforts to the contrary, I have been unable to convince Mike to stay in the department and continue to his career as a criminologist. He is coming up for tenure and promotion to associate professor this year which

*(second page intentionally omitted to obscure
the identity of the author)*

CHAPTER 10

When You Come to a Fork
in the Road, Take It

Originally published in 2007 as "Life and How to Live It, Part X."

In the introduction, I stated that one of Mike's transformations was his becoming a public figure. In the previous chapter, we saw that his pro-life advocacy helped fuel his public speaking. In this article, he indicates how he decided to become a columnist.

You may recall that I had a less-than-stellar record as a high school student. It took a while for me to get things going but, as soon as I gathered momentum, I had a hard time slowing down.

My first year as a college professor [1993] demanded a lot of hard work. I had to prepare for several classes I hadn't taught previously. But by plugging away nightly, I was able to get through the year with flying colors. I somehow registered the highest teaching evaluations in my department after only one semester.

During my second year as a professor, I had to focus on research. I knew that if I spun a couple of articles off my dissertation and wrote or co-wrote a couple of "new" articles, I would be a lock to get tenure. Things worked out well. My department voted unanimously to grant me tenure after just four years and two months on the job.

Instead of taking a rest after getting tenure, I started to study for the LSAT. The following month I took the test and scored high enough to get into all three of the schools I had been considering seriously. Then, in one of the most foolish moves of my life, I turned down a scholarship offer from The University of Georgia School of Law. I later accepted an offer from UNC School of Law and enrolled in the fall of 1998.

For the first few months, I studied diligently—an average of about five hours a night. But, for some reason, I started to have serious attention problems in class by the time November rolled around. The Clinton impeachment scandal was dominating the political shows on both radio and television. But unfortunately, I didn't have enough time to weigh in on the serious issues that confronted our nation during that time.

As Thanksgiving approached, my problems staying awake in class were getting worse. I was becoming very bored with law school in general. I also found it hard to take UNC Law seriously, as the school seemed to offer more seminars dealing with transgendered rights than seminars dealing with serious legal issues. So, I decided to take a weekend off and head out of town to catch up on some shopping.

As I was looking through some books at the mall, I came across *Sexual McCarthyism* by Alan Dershowitz. As I was holding the book, I had an immediate realization about my life and where it was headed. I knew I did not ever want to practice law. I knew I wanted to teach college and become an irreverent columnist and author, much like Alan Dershowitz.

I knew I had taken a wrong turn in my career by pursuing a law degree I would never put to use.

As you can imagine, the months that followed my decision to return to academia were depressing. After all, I had wasted a year's salary in order to find out what I did not want to do with my life. I had sold an awesome row house built in 1912, which was the coolest place I'd ever lived. And, to make matters worse, I was forced to end a relationship with a girl I was falling in love with over the summer preceding my enrollment in law school.

For months on end, I sat up late at night staring at the ceiling and asking myself why I had not just slowed down after getting tenure so I could just enjoy life for a few years. After falling asleep I would often wake up in a pool of sweat thinking about all that I had lost in the preceding months. Sometimes, it was the money. Sometimes, it was the house. Sometimes, it was the girl.

I didn't realize just how far I had been set back financially until I went back to Wilmington to look for another house. I could not find anything I liked as much as my old 1912 row house. So, I settled for an overpriced, cheaply built, and utterly boring town home near the beach.

When I moved in during the summer of 1999, I was feeling pretty sorry for myself. I was a wannabe pundit with no book deal, no column, and no radio or television show. I simply did not have a platform. I only had debt.

Seven years (to the day) after I moved back to Wilmington, I got a very surprising phone call from my agent, D.J. Snell. He told me that Penguin U.S.A. was offering me a contract for my book *Feminists Say the Darndest Things*: the advance and bonuses totaling $10,000 more than the salary I had lost that year I was in law school. So, after I got off the phone, I bought a six-pack and headed to my back deck to do some serious thinking. Naturally, this was done while I watched the bug zapper.

As I was sitting on the back deck, I thought about the 1912 row house I had sold in 1998. It had not appreciated that much since I moved away. But the town house I bought to replace it ended up doing quite well. In fact, after someone decided to build the shopping center next door, its value went up enough in just six months to recoup that year's loss of salary that once had me feeling so depressed.

And the story gets even better. I took the money I made on that town home and rolled it over into a house twice as big. That investment paid off to the tune of an appreciation over the next two years that was three times the salary I lost by taking the year off. Oddly, I ended up making a lot of money I never would have made had I not taken the year off to head to UNC School of Law.

I guess that, unlike my other "Life and How to Live It" articles, this one needs no bold letters to highlight the main point. Just read it again the next time you think God has abandoned you. And realize that your best days may be ahead of you still.

For Further Reading: Romans 8:18-28

GOD HAS NEVER ABANDONED ME.
QUITE THE OPPOSITE ACTUALLY. ⸻

In case you don't have a Bible handy:

[18] I consider that our present sufferings are not worth comparing with the glory that will be revealed in us. [19] For the creation waits in eager expectation for the children of God to be revealed. [20] For the creation was subjected to frustration, not by its own choice, but by the will of the one who subjected it, in hope [21] that the creation itself will be

liberated from its bondage to decay and brought into the freedom and glory of the children of God.

²² We know that the whole creation has been groaning as in the pains of childbirth right up to the present time. ²³ Not only so, but we ourselves, who have the first fruits of the Spirit, groan inwardly as we wait eagerly for our adoption to sonship, the redemption of our bodies. ²⁴ For in this hope we were saved. But hope that is seen is no hope at all. Who hopes for what they already have? ²⁵ But if we hope for what we do not yet have, we wait for it patiently.

²⁶ In the same way, the Spirit helps us in our weakness. We do not know what we ought to pray for, but the Spirit himself intercedes for us through wordless groans. ²⁷ And he who searches our hearts knows the mind of the Spirit, because the Spirit intercedes for God's people in accordance with the will of God.

²⁸ And we know that in all things God works for the good of those who love him, who have been called according to his purpose.

Romans 8:18 – "I consider that our present sufferings are not worth comparing with the glory that will be revealed in us."

Mike is now in that glory. Not long after he passed, I was shown a brief but moving vision of my brother and our parents. They were simply smiling at each other. There were no words, but I felt the emotion. All anxiety, fear, worries, sadness, etc., were gone and replaced with peace and contentment. I know that God was telling me that I don't have to worry about them and letting me know that is what I can look forward to.

THE UNIVERSITY OF NORTH CAROLINA AT WILMINGTON

MARVIN K. MOSS
*Provost and Vice Chancellor
For Academic Affairs*

September 16, 1996

Mike S. Adams
Department of Sociology and Anthropology
UNCW

Dear Dr. Adams:

As you may know, the Legislature designated a 4.5% raise for faculty to be based on merit. The Legislature also voted an additional 1/2% to be used to recognize and reward those faculty demonstrating substantial teaching excellence. At UNCW we chose to use that 1/2% to recognize a number of faculty with a $2,000 permanent addition to their salary in addition to any merit raise increases. I am most pleased to inform you that you are one of those faculty recommended and selected to receive these monies. It is impossible to fully compensate faculty like you who give so much of your time, energy, and expertise to students but, on behalf of the university, I thank you for all that you do and hope that this permanent adjustment to your salary, which will be reflected in your paycheck starting in September, express, at least in part, our recognition of and gratitude for your work.

Congratulations and my best personal wishes for a most successful 1996-97 academic year.

Sincerely,

Marvin K. Moss

CHAPTER 11

~~~~~

The End of Affirmative Action

Originally published in 2006.

Before we leave the "Learning" section and move to the "Teaching" section, there is one more transformation we still need to reference, and that is the liberal to conservative political transformation, which Mike discusses below.

For years, people have asked me why I switched from being a left-wing Democrat to a right-wing Republican. When I'm not in the mood to talk, I give a one-word response: reality. When I'm feeling more verbose, I give a two-word response: affirmative action.

Affirmative action in theory bears no resemblance to affirmative action in reality. The theory part was taught to me as a doctoral student in a sociology department in the late 1980s and early 1990s. Most of the academic rhetoric focused on what affirmative action isn't.

But sometimes, my professors would calm lingering doubts by saying what affirmative action is; namely, that it is both temporary and a tiebreaker. Those are really the only affirmative statements I've ever heard about affirmative action.

But then I graduated from college and finally had an opportunity to experience affirmative action in reality. Those early experiences, like the later ones, were uniformly negative.

As a young Ph.D. student, I was told by a department chair at Memphis State (now the University of Memphis) that, due to race, I had no chance in a head-to-head contest with the only other interviewee, a black male. He was honest enough to say that they were under too much pressure from Human Resources to give me a fair shake.

So, I withdrew from that interview only to learn a year later that I couldn't fully escape the overt racial discrimination of affirmative action. In my first informal recruitment meeting as a professor in the University of North Carolina system, I listened to a social worker object to an applicant on the grounds that he was a "little too white male."

Of course, it should come as no surprise that people engage in racial discrimination in hiring when they are specifically asked to do so by Human Resources. But what is surprising about affirmative action is the extent to which it encourages discrimination along the lines of other variables not classified as "allowable" under official policies.

I have simply lost count of the number of times over the years that my colleagues have brought factors such as political affiliation and religion into discussions of job applicants.

Objections such as "He's too religious" or "He's too much of a family man" or "Her husband plays too dominant a role in their marriage" are simply indefensible. And it is worth asking whether such criteria would be so casually considered if Human Resources did not open a Pandora's box by deeming some discrimination to be an "acceptable" means to a desirable end.

But the discussion of affirmative action should by no means focus on the bad results it produces for white males like me. The real tragedy is its negative impact on the groups it purports to help. The effect is one I describe with a phrase called the "Reverse Roger Bannister Effect."

When Roger Bannister broke the four-minute mile in 1954, a whole class of people—not a race but those who run them—realized for the first time that a seemingly insurmountable goal could be achieved. So, naturally, others started breaking the four-minute barrier left and right just as soon as the bar of achievement was raised by Bannister.

That is precisely the opposite of what is happening with affirmative action. By lowering the bar and (in the short-term) making things easier for minorities, we guarantee persistent gaps in achievement. President Bush calls this the "soft bigotry" of low expectations. I prefer to call it the "hard reality" of low expectations.

Affirmative action is also an embarrassment for minorities who do not need or want to be measured by a lower standard. A black female student I taught in 1993 summed it up best by saying that although she had been admitted to college on the basis of outstanding grades and test scores, no one believed her. Whites just assumed she was there because of affirmative action. Once a class of people is given credit for something its members did not achieve, individuals in that class forfeit credit for the things they actually did.

I also look back on certain experiences and realize that affirmative action degrades whole institutions, not just individuals.

Twice, our department has flown in a white candidate under the mistaken belief that he or she was black. But we cannot accuse these candidates of lying about their race just to get an interview. In fact, we lie to them when we print "The

UNC system does not discriminate on the basis of race" on every application. And I wonder how we still have the moral authority to punish students who plagiarize or cheat.

But maybe widespread lying is the best solution to the problem of affirmative action. If our students would all wake up one day and decide to start checking the box for "African American" on every university form, our affirmative action programs would break down altogether. Then maybe we could replace "race consciousness" with the colorblindness Martin Luther King envisioned.

Mike elaborates on his political transformation in a 2005 article:

My political transformation was perhaps even more gradual than my religious transformation. It was more of an issue-by-issue conversion. Some examples follow:

After a fellow fraternity member and his girlfriend were abducted by an armed assailant and murdered during my last year in college, I decided to abandon my support of gun control.

After learning in graduate school that affirmative action did not involve quotas and reverse discrimination—that it was merely a tiebreaker for equally qualified applicants (and a temporary program to boot)—I went to work in the academy and saw how it really worked. Confronted with the truth of affirmative action, I had to abandon my support of what was clearly a permanent and discriminatory policy.

After seeing a film of an unborn child yawning, rubbing his eyes, and playfully rolling around in his mother's womb, I realized that the fetus becomes a person long before birth and long after the Supreme Court allows it to be aborted. Therefore, I had to abandon my support of abortion rights.

Eventually, I woke up and realized that I had more in common with the Republicans than I did with the Democrats. I was also beginning to develop a new appreciation for moral absolutism, which would help to revive me spiritually.

*Upper row, far right, wearing an Elton
John "Capitan Fantastic" shirt.*

*Visit from our New Orleans friends, the
Gause family. Mike far right.*

HALLOWEEN NITEBUIIY3
WE GOT - SCAREY DRINKS
SCAREY ANNE AND MIKE
AND A DARK ROOM

1992

2012, at our parents' house in The Woodlands.

2019, Mississippi, after mother's funeral.
Photo credit: Jasmine Richards.

Painting by Anna Stonestreet, of the Manitou Incline, one of Mike's favorite spots.

Frank Turek, Jake Hibbs, J. Warner Wallace, Mike.

Mike and Marquietta.

Memorial Service, Westport Baptist Church, Denver,
North Carolina. Photo credit: Brittany Boland.

The Mike S. Adams Memorial Studio at Summit Ministries in Manitou Springs, Colorado, is an historic building that was totally rehabbed and converted into a state-of-the-art recording studio largely with donations from Mike's friends, family, and fans. This ensures that Mike's legacy lives on.

PART TWO

Teaching

PATRICIA L. LEONARD
Vice Chancellor
For Student Affairs

May 2, 2004

Dr. Mike S. Adams
Sociology & Criminal Justice
College Of Arts & Sciences

mike,
Dear Dr. Adams,

On behalf of the Division of Students Affairs, I wish to offer my most sincere congratulations for being recognized by one or more of the students in the May 2004 graduating class for having made a difference in their lives. I would also like to share with you comments that were made on your behalf.

Each semester, the Division of Student Affairs asks graduating seniors to identify faculty or staff members who have had a significant impact on them while attending UNCW. Our university is extremely fortunate to have such a caring and genuinely committed person as you working with our students to make their experience successful and memorable. We believe that these connections with students are essential to building a strong university community. This notable accomplishment has been shared with the chancellor, vice chancellors, deans, directors and department chairs.

We are proud of our university community and especially those individuals who engage our students on a personal level. Again, I thank you for your commitment.

Best wishes,

Pat

Patricia L. Leonard
Vice Chancellor for Student Affairs

PLL/ lvk

Dr. Mike S. Adams
Sociology & Criminal Justice

- He has the best stories! He showed me that you can have loads of fun and still achieve success.

- He was my first college professor and he really seemed to care about his students. I have had him for a lot of classes and he is just a great teacher. He is not afraid to say what he believes and I really respect that. He is just easy to talk to and get along with. He is a great teacher and person for this university.

- He is an excellent teacher and showed genuine concern for all his students both inside and outside the classroom.

- He helped me gain direction, enthusiasm, and intensity in my academic pursuits both through his engaging courses and personal attention. For all of this, I thank you.

- If not for him, I would have given up a long time ago.

- He made learning fun and provided me with the knowledge to succeed in the real world.

- He advised me throughout my college career.

CHAPTER 12

The UNCW Classes

At this point, we have read about many of Mike's life experiences and the transformations that resulted. Now, we shift our focus to his teaching. Mike loved to teach, and he was exceptional at it, in and out of the classroom. He had a huge impact on many people, as we shall see later on in the "Remembrances" chapter.

Mike's syllabi were originally more simple and less funny, but they were enhanced over time as he built upon his teaching and life experiences.

Mike prepared meticulously for everything. In his library, I found many books that he used for preparing his classes, especially on the Till and Simpson cases (see below). It seemed as if he owned every book on those cases! In fact, Mike was planning to write a book called Seven Trials: How Famous Cases Reflect and Shape American Culture, *which I assume would have been based on his "Trials of the Century" class.*

In 2015, Mike wrote: Today, a student interviewed me and asked which of the five courses I teach is my favorite. I told her it was a five-way tie. I thoroughly enjoy everything I do.

CRM 105 - INTRODUCTION TO CRIMINAL JUSTICE

READ THIS SYLLABUS BEFORE YOU RETURN TO THIS CLASS! Last semester, I was peppered all semester long with basic questions that were answered in the syllabus. If you fail to read your syllabus and ask me a question about something in the syllabus, I will do three things: 1) Run off a syllabus for you. 2) Hand it to you in class. 3) Deduct three points from your final average and give them to someone who read his syllabus.

Note: This class is seventy-five minutes long. Go potty before class, not during class. If you walk out during class, I will assume you have gone out in the hall to use your cell phone. This is a reasonable assumption since people never walked out of class to go potty until I banned cell phones.

Another note: Don't tell me you have to leave class early to go to the doctor or feed the parking meter (or anything else for that matter). This is not an open house. Stay for the whole class or don't bother showing up.

A final note before we get down to business: These notes are a part of the syllabus. Disregard them and I will be giving you a new syllabus.

Books:
Kevin Cook. *Kitty Genovese: The Murder, The Bystanders, The Crime That Changed America*. James A. Inciardi. *Criminal Justice* (9th edition)
Optional: Marcus Felson. *Crime and Everyday Life*.

Course Objectives: The primary objective of this course will be to introduce the student to the field of criminal justice. Criminal justice refers to the structure, function, and processes of agencies that are supposed to manage and control crime and criminal offenders. Criminal justice differs from criminology in that it focuses less on the causes of crime and more on responding to crime.

Grading: Four multiple-format tests will be given. Each will be given equal weight. One will be dropped.

Note: When I go over tests in class you may disagree with my designation of some answers as incorrect. Do not try to argue your point during class. Instead, make your point in writing and slip it under my door. I will review each and every challenge and notify you as to my "ruling" on the matter as soon as possible.

DO NOT COME TO SEE ME BEFORE OR AFTER YOUR ABSENCE WITH AN EXPLANATION. I WILL NOT TAKE ROLL IN THIS CLASS. I WILL ALLOW THOSE WHO SHOULD NOT BE IN COLLEGE TO WEED THEMSELVES OUT OF THE STUDENT POPULATION. (If you insist on giving me an excuse anyway then I will give you something: a brand-new syllabus hot off the presses).

Course Outline: This course will be broken down into four sections. You will be tested at the end of each section. The reading assignments and major questions or topics to be addressed in each section are as follows:

SECTION I Inciardi, Chapters 1, 3 and 4.

How Do We Approach Crime in America? The distinction between liberal and conservative crime control ideology is discussed.

Just What Is Crime Anyway? Crimes against the person, property crimes, victimless crimes, organized crime, and white-collar crime will be discussed.

Problems Associated with Measuring Crime. Almost everyone says that crime is on the rise and that the U.S. has more crime that any other "civilized" nation. But how do they really know? This topic is explored by looking at the strengths and weaknesses of the UCR, NCVS, and Self-Report studies of crime and deviance.

TEST I (Date TBA)

SECTION II Inciardi, Chapters 5 and 8.

Fundamental and Formal Constitutional Rights. We will talk mostly about the nationalization of the Bill of Rights.

Issues in Criminal Due Process. We will focus mainly of the rules of search and seizure.

TEST II (Date TBA)

SECTION III Inciardi, Chapters 11, 12, 13, and 18.

Judges, Prosecutors, and Other Performers at the Bar of Justice. The focus here is on the right to counsel and several important Supreme Court Decisions. *Powell v. Alabama, Johnson v. Zerbst, Betts v. Brady, Gideon v. Wainwright, and Argersinger v. Hamlin.*

The Business of the Court. I will talk about types of evidence. I will also take a few minutes to talk about the Simpson verdict. Specifically, I will talk about why he is guilty well beyond any conceivable doubt and why the jury failed to arrive at such a simple and obvious conclusion.

Limitations on the Death Penalty in America. Five important death penalty cases are discussed.

The Juvenile Justice System. There will be a brief overview of the juvenile justice system plus a lengthy discussion of *In Re Gault and New Jersey v. T.L.O.*

SECTION IV Cook and Felson.

Crime Causation and the Defense of Insanity. We will use Cook's book to talk about the Kitty Genovese case.

Routine Activities and Crime Prevention. We will use Felson's book to talk about how Genovese's rape and murder could have easily been prevented. Hint: It isn't the fault of "society."

Progressive Theories of Crime. If time permits, we will watch *Boyz in the Hood.* I will show how the film demonstrates the major progressive theories of crime causation and why they are all wrong.

Final Exam: Consult schedule.

Course Learning Objectives: 1. Expand student understanding of the role of the Bill of Rights in our system of justice. 2. Develop student's ability to analyze and evaluate landmark Supreme Court decisions. 3. Increase student knowledge of fundamental differences in judicial philosophy and crime control policy.

CRM 381 – CRIMINAL PROCEDURE

Required Reading: Israel and LaFave's *Criminal Procedure in a Nutshell*, 9th edition.

Course Objectives: This course was once taught as the latter half of Criminal Law and Procedure. I am really pleased that we divided that course into two separate courses: 1) CRM 380 "Criminal Law" and 2) CRM 381 "Criminal Procedure." The two are distinctively different and the latter is continuously growing.

If you drive across the United States of America on I-40 (follow the sign that says "Barstow, CA, 2554 miles"!), you will encounter numerous changes in the criminal law. The rules for a serious felony could change a half a dozen times before you reach the Golden State. Not so with regard to criminal procedure. Back in the 1960s, the Supreme Court nationalized most of the rules governing procedure. You learned about some of those changes in the "intro" course (CRM 105). You will learn about those changes in greater detail. You will also learn about other changes that time restraints kept your professor from covering in CRM 105.

This course will focus primarily on the exclusionary rules for the Fourth Amendment, the Fifth Amendment, and the Sixth Amendment. The Fourth Amendment will receive more attention than the Fifth Amendment. The Fifth Amendment will receive more attention than the Sixth Amendment. If you know anyone in law enforcement, you will understand why the amendments are not given equal treatment.

Of course, this is not just a class for prospective law enforcement officers. It is also a class for prospective law students. Even if you do not fit into either category, you will benefit from this class. Citizens need to know their rights. The surest way a government can deprive citizens of their rights is to ensure they never knew them in the first place.

Course Activities: I will talk about a lot of cases this semester. You may be called on to brief one or two of them. I will explain how that is to be done (in our first class meeting). When you present your case briefs you will be a part of the dialogue about the case. Whenever someone else presents a case brief you will just listen. Take good notes.

Grading: There will be three tests, each worth 33.3 percent of your grade. Tests are all true/false questions. But they are also essay in the sense that you must explain all false answers.

Note: I will take attendance this semester. If you miss three classes, it is no big deal. If you miss four classes, I will attach a minus to your final grade. For every additional absence I will deduct a letter grade. You get to use these three absences whenever you want, regardless of the reason. It is never necessary for you to email a doctor's note or an explanation of your personal issues. **DO NOT EVER DO THAT**. If you do, I will assume you have not bothered reading the syllabus. That will lead me to believe that you are not a responsible, mature adult.

Course Learning Objectives: 1. To teach you criminal procedure. 2. To teach you that the "course objectives" they force us to list on the syllabus are generally meaningless.

Schedule of Topics and Assignments:

Meeting One: Discussion of syllabus.
Meeting Two: Read Chapter One. *Hurtado v. Cal.* (1884), *Palko v. Conn.* (1937), *Ker v. Cal.* (1963).
Meeting Three: Read Chapter Two. *Weeks v. U.S.* (1914), *Mapp v. Ohio* (1961), *Katz v. U.S.* (1967).

Meeting Four: *Kyllo v. U.S.* (2001), *Cal. v. Ciraolo* (1986), *Fla. V. Riley* (1989).

Meeting Five: *Cal. v. Greenwood* (1988), *Ill. v. Gates* (1983), *Coolidge v. N.H.* (1971).

Meeting Six: *Connally v. Ga.* (1977), *Atwater v. City of Lago Vista* (2001), *Gerstein v. Pugh* (1975).

Meeting Seven: *Tenn. V. Garner* (1985). *Chimel v. Cal.* (1969). *Payton v. N.Y.* (1980).

Meeting Eight: *Welsh v. Wis.* (1984), *Steagald v. U.S.* (1981). *Ariz. v. Hicks* (1987).

Meeting Nine: Review.

Meeting Ten: Test.

Meeting Eleven: *Ariz. v. Gant* (2009), *Carroll v. U.S.* (1925), *Cal. v. Carney* (1985).

Meeting Twelve: *Terry v. Ohio* (1968), *Ill. V. Wardlow* (2000), *Adams. V. Williams* (1972).

Meeting Thirteen: *Cal. v. Hodari D.* (1991), *Minn. v. Dickerson* (1993). *Del. v. Prouse* (1979).

Meeting Fourteen: *City of Indianapolis v. Edmond* (2000), *N.J. v. T.L.O.* (1985), *U.S. v. Matlock* (1974).

Meeting Fifteen: *Ga. v. Randolph* (2006), *Ill. v. Rodriguez* (1990), *Olmstead v. U.S.* (1928).

Meeting Sixteen: Read Chapter Three. *Hoffa v. U.S.* (1966), *U.S. v. White* (1971), *Brown v. Miss.* (1936).

Meeting Seventeen: Read Chapter Four. *Malloy v. Hogan* (1964), *Massiah v. U.S.* (1964), *Escobedo v. Ill.* (1964).

Meeting Eighteen: Review.

Meeting Nineteen: Test.

Meeting Twenty: *Miranda v. Ariz.* (1966), *R.I. v. Innis* (1980), *Ill. V. Perkins* (1990).

Meeting Twenty-One: *Pa. v. Muniz* (1990), *N.Y. v. Quarles* (1984), *N.C. v. Butler* (1979).

Meeting Twenty-Two: Read Chapter Six. *U.S. v. Leon* (1984), *Silverthorne v. U.S.* (1920), *Walder v. U.S.* (1954).

Meeting Twenty-Three: *Harris v. N.Y.* (1971), *Powell v. Ala.* (1932), *Johnson v. Zerbst* (1938).

Meeting Twenty-Four: Read Chapter Seven. *Betts v. Brady* (1942), *Gideon v. Wainwright* (1963), *Argersinger v. Hamlin* (1972).

Meeting Twenty-Five: *Douglas v. Cal.* (1963), *Ake. V. Okla.* (1985), *Mempa v. Rhay* (1976).

Meeting Twenty-Six: *Johnson v. Avery* (1969), *Bounds v. Smith* (1977), *Faretta v. Cal.* (1975).

Meeting Twenty-Seven: Review.

Meeting Twenty-Eight: Test.

CRM 385 – LAW OF EVIDENCE

Required Reading: *Federal Rules of Evidence (Tenth Edition), by Graham* You will be counted absent every day that your book is not visibly displayed when I call the roll. It is that essential.

Course Objectives: This course is intended to introduce student to rules of evidence that apply to both criminal and civil cases. In this class, we will focus almost exclusively on the Federal Rules of Evidence. In addition to dictating admissibility in federal cases, these rules have been adopted by about forty states. North Carolina follows these rules more closely than most states. In other words, a person practicing law in North Carolina—civil or criminal, state or federal court—must become familiar with these rules. You do not need to have any interest in practicing law in order to benefit from knowledge of evidence law. Those interested in law enforcement undoubtedly foresee testifying some day in a court of law. These rules will impact the substance and presentation of that testimony. If you are unsure of what you intend to do, you will still benefit from a tremendous intellectual challenge.

Course Activities: I will usually spend Mondays going over new rules. I will usually spend Wednesdays talking about hypothetical problems that will test your understanding of the rules.

Grading: There will be three tests, each worth 33 percent of your grade. The good news is that all three tests will be in true/false format. The bad news is that you must explain why an answer you marked false is false.

Test One (mid to late September) will cover: General Relevance and Privileges.
Test Two (late October) will cover: Witness Examination/ Impeachment, Expert Witnesses.
Test Three (see final exam schedule) will cover: Hearsay.

Attendance: You may miss class three times. I will count three points off your final average for each additional absence.

Learning Objectives: The fact that I am required by government bureaucrats to list "learning objectives" in addition to the "course objectives" I have already listed infuriates me. Ergo, my sole "learning objective" for the semester is to teach you that a "learning objective" is a meaningless concept devised by government bureaucrats in order to create more government jobs because they lack the skills required to make them employable in the private sector.

CRM 395 – THE FIRST AMENDMENT AND CRIME

Required Reading: *Unlearning Liberty* by Greg Lukianoff. *Hate: Why We Should Resist It with Free Speech, Not Censorship* by Nadine Strossen.

Course Objectives: This course was originally supposed to be called "The First Amendment and Original Intent." Then, in response to an emergency, I was asked to re-tool it into a senior seminar. In response to my disdain for the accreditation bureaucracy, I decided to make it a special topics class. (Because it is no longer a capstone class, the accreditation Nazis no longer control my course content. Fitting response for a First Amendment advocate, is it not?). It is now an overview of First Amendment cases, all of which are crime related. It begins with a discussion of the first important free speech cases in American history, which were necessitated by the over-zealousness of the Wilson administration during World War I. From there it moves into more contemporary problems associated with the criminalization of obscenity and "expressive conduct." Before the semester ends, we will get into some contemporary issues such hate crimes legislation and penalty-enhancement statutes. This may be the most interesting and relevant course you ever take as a student at UNCW. I do not say that for lack of humility. (See my forthcoming book, *Ten Steps to Humility: And How I Made It in Seven.*). But, seriously, I'm just working with really interesting and sometimes explosive material. Over the course of the semester, we will all gain a greater understanding of a very complex area of constitutional law.

Class Activities and Grading: I will talk about a lot of cases this semester. You will each brief several of them. I will explain how that is to be done (in our first class meeting). When you present your case briefs you will be a part of the dialogue about the case. Whenever someone else presents a case brief you will just listen. Take good notes as the cases are covered on the exams. Your grade will be based upon your three tests, which are worth ten points each, and your case briefs, which are worth five points each. I will simply take your points earned, divide by number of points possible, and grade on a 10 percent-point scale.

Note that I will take attendance this semester. **If you miss two classes, it is no big deal. If you miss three classes, I will attach a minus to your final grade. For every additional absence I will deduct a letter grade.** It is never necessary for you to email a doctor's note or an explanation of your personal issues. **DO NOT EVER DO THAT**. If you do, I will assume you have not bothered reading the syllabus. That will lead me to believe that you are not a responsible, mature adult.

Course Learning Objectives: To foster an understanding of the danger of the government assuming control of speech. This includes, but is not limited to, forcing professors to speak against their will by including useless learning objectives in their course syllabi.

Class Outline:

Meeting One: Introduction to the class, explanation of syllabus, assignment of briefs.

Meeting Two: *New York Times v. United States (1971). Gitlow v. New York (1925). Schenck v. United States (1919). Whitney v. California (1927). Chaplinsky v. New Hampshire (1942).* Story time: The Sexual Horoscopes.

Meeting Three: *RAV v. Minnesota (1992). Virginia v. Black (2003). Simon & Schuster v. New York Crime Victims Board (1991). Renton v. Playtime Theatres (1986). United States v. O'Brien (1968).* Story time: In Dedication to An Undivided Humanity.

Meeting Four: *Hill v. Colorado (2000). Board of Air Commissioners v. Jews for Jesus (1987). Krishna v. Lee (1992). Osborne v. Ohio (1990). Brandenburg v. Ohio (1969).* Story time: The SAE Act.

Meeting Five: *Cohen v. California (1971). Terminiello v. Chicago (1949). Gregory v. Chicago (1969). Roth v. United States (1957). Jacobellis v. Ohio (1964).* Story Time: The Queen of Anal Sex.

Meeting Six: *John Cleland's Memoirs v. Massachusetts (1966). Miller v. California (1973). Stanley v. Georgia (1969). New York Times v. Sullivan (1964). Hustler Magazine v. Falwell (1988).* Story time: UNCG Hates Free Speech (and libertarian Gothic chicks, too).

Meeting Seven: *Texas v. Johnson (1989). Wisconsin v. Mitchell (1993). NAACP v. Alabama (1958). West Virginia v. Barnette (1943). Wisconsin v. Southworth (2000).* Story time: Ruth, Orit, and the Twinkie Toting Female Dogs.

Meeting Eight: *Boy Scouts of America v. Dale (2000). Hazelwood v. Kuhlmeier (1988). Rankin v. McPherson (1987). Garcetti v. Ceballos (2005). Rosenberger v. Rector (1995).* Story time: The ACLU, the Mountaineers, and the Six-foot Walking Vagina.

Meeting Nine: Test One.

Meeting Ten: Chapters 1-5 in *Unlearning Liberty*. Story time: The Dean, the Senator, and the Free Speech Bill (or how censorship backfired in the school of journalism).

Meeting Eleven: Chapters 6-10 in *Unlearning Liberty*. Story time: How I got micro-aggressed at the University of New Hampshire.

Meeting Twelve: Test Two.

Meeting Thirteen: Chapters 1-9 in *Hate*. Story time: The Heckler's Veto: From Massachusetts to Montana.

Meeting Fourteen: Test Three.

CRM 425 – TRIALS OF THE CENTURY

Required Books:

Outrage by Vincent Bugliosi or *Fatal Vision* by Joe McGinnis.
Summer for the Gods by Edward Larson or *Reversal of Fortune* Alan Dershowitz.
Emmett Till: The Murder That Shocked the World and Propelled the Civil Rights Movement by Devery S. Anderson or *Helter Skelter* by Vincent Bugliosi.
American Heiress by Jeffrey Toobin or *Gosnell* by Ann McElhinney and Phelim McAleer

Note: In order to be counted present you must be present with one of the books you are supposed to be reading for that particular course section. It must be prominently displayed on your desk during the roll call. I will explain and remind periodically. Choose your four books and order immediately. I will not adjust the class schedule to accommodate your lack of planning.

Optional Study Materials:
The Beatles *White* Album.
[Charles Manson claimed to be inspired by this album, especially the song "Helter Skelter."]

Course Objectives:
In 1904, Supreme Court Justice Oliver Wendell Holmes, Jr., stated, "Great cases, like hard cases, make bad law. For great cases are called great, not by reason of their real importance in shaping the law of the future, but because of some accident of immediate overwhelming interest which appeals to the feelings and distorts the judgment." Indeed, many great cases in recent memory have evoked strong emotional responses. Sadly, many impressions of the current state of our criminal justice system (and many suggestions for its future) are based upon cursory knowledge of popular trials. In this class, we will

look at some of these popular trials in depth. We will see that these cases rarely represent the true state of our criminal justice system. They are unusual cases, which should not be used to make judgments about how our system should be modified. Note that this course seeks to analyze important *criminal* trials, all of which took place during the twentieth century. The cases covered will vary from semester to semester and may occasionally include cases from the nineteenth century. Thus, the course title is not meant to refer to a particular historical period. It merely reflects the importance of these individual cases. Actually, over thirty trials were dubbed "trial of the century" by the media during the Twentieth Century. Unfortunately, we cannot cover them all.

The basis for selecting these particular trials is that they reflect important constitutional, social, and even psychological issues. Though they are not representative trials, they are all important. For example, the Simpson murder trial revealed much about the current state of race relations in America. It also stimulated calls for various reforms in the legal system. The same can be said of the Hinckley case, which started a movement to abolish the insanity defense in the United States. While stopping short of abolishing the insanity defense, it did impose new limitations on insanity claims. Among those were new restrictions on psychiatric testimony concerning ultimate issues in criminal trials. You will undoubtedly notice as the semester unfolds that few of these cases actually resulted in great legal changes. Often, they merely reflected social issues outside of the legal realm. The Scopes case provides a good example in that regard.

Grading Scheme:
You will all take four tests.

Test one will cover the Simpson trial or the Jeffrey MacDonald trial.

Test two will cover the Von Bulow trial, or the Scopes trial.

Test three will cover the Manson trial or the Emmett Till trial.

Test four (final exam) will cover the Hearst trial or the Gosnell trial.

Each test will be equally weighted. Ten percent grade cutoffs are employed.

Note: I will take attendance this semester. If you miss a class or two it is no big deal. However, for every additional absence I will deduct a letter grade.

LECTURE TOPICS:

Week 1 Course Introduction.

Week 2 O.J. Simpson Saga: Reasonable doubts from the defense perspective.

Week 3 O.J. Simpson (continued): Unreasonable doubts from the eyes of a prosecutor.

Week 4 O.J. Simpson (continued): Unreasonable doubts from the eyes of a prosecutor.

Week 5 Jeffrey Macdonald: The inescapable power of circumstantial evidence.

Week 6 Test One.

Week 7 John Thomas Scopes: What really happened before history was rewritten by Hollywood.

Week 8 The Claus von Bülow Trial, Appeal, and Retrial: The best defense money can buy.

Week 9 Test Two.

Week 10 The Manson family trial: Easily provable murders with a nearly un-provable motive.

Week 11 The Emmett Till lynching: A complex ordeal that history has oversimplified ... to everyone's detriment.

Week 12 Test Three

Week 13 The Patty Hearst Trial: The worst defense money can buy.

Week 14 The Gosnell Trial: You probably have never heard of the nation's most notorious serial killer. Even some professors pretend not to know this man's name. It is shameful. I'll explain.

Final exam (consult schedule).

Course Learning Objectives:

1. Expand student understanding of the role that great criminal trials have played in shaping public opinion of our system of justice
2. Develop student ability to analyze and critique judicial rulings and trial strategy decisions in numerous major American criminal cases
3. Increase student knowledge of the fact that "course learning objectives" are mandated and do not in any way enhance student learning. They merely demonstrate that American higher education is held captive by bureaucratic interest groups that do nothing for students and merely irritate faculty and distract them from their more important duties.

I am presenting these classes in numerical order, except for this one. I saved it for last because this is the last class Mike created. On 9/2/2019, Mike posted: "I am nearly done with the syllabus for CRM 110 Issues in Criminal Justice. The course has no prerequisites and can thus be taken by anyone at UNCW. Students will read

Thomas Sowell, John Lott, Heather McDonald, and a host of other conservative and libertarian readings. This is my response to left-wing indoctrination at UNCW. All 17,000 students need a course like this. I begin offering it in the spring of 2020."

CRM 110 – ISSUES IN CRIMINAL JUSTICE

Required Books:
Kevin Cook. *Kitty Genovese: The Murder, The Bystanders, The Crime That Changed America.*
K.C. Johnson and Stuart Taylor. *The Campus Rape Frenzy: The Attack On Due Process At America's Universities.*
Mike Lee. *Our Lost Constitution: The Willful Subversion of America's Founding Document.*
Heather MacDonald. *The War on Cops: How The Attack on Law and Order Makes Everyone Less Safe.*

Optional Books:
Stephen Baskerville. *Taken Into Custody: The War Against Fathers, Marriage, and the Family.*
Dave Cullen. *Columbine.*
Marcus Felson. *Crime And Everyday Life: Insight and Implications For Society.*
Mollie Hemingway. *Justice On Trial: The Kavanaugh Confirmation and The Future Of The Supreme Court.*
Stephen Jimenez. *The Book of Matt: Hidden Truths About The Murder of Matthew Shepard.*
Mark Levin. *Men In Black: How The Supreme Court Is Destroying America.*
Thomas Sowell. *The Vision of the Anointed: Self-Congratulation as A Basis For Social Policy.*
John R. Lott, Jr. *More Guns, Less Crime: Understanding Crime and Gun Control Laws.*

Stuart Taylor and K.C. Johnson. *Until Proven Innocent: Political Correctness and The Shameful Injustices Of The Duke Lacrosse Rape Case.*

William Wilbanks. *The Myth of A Racist Criminal Justice System.*

Required Movie: *Boyz in the Hood.*
Optional Movie: *Unplanned.*

Course Objectives: This course is a reasoned response to systematic academic malpractice. For far too long, professors at this university have been using the classroom as a forum for the dissemination of political views that are often only loosely relate to the subject matter of the course they are teaching. Actually, it is unfair to use the term "forum," which implies that multiple points of view are being exchanged. Particularly within the so-called social sciences and the humanities, one-party classrooms tend to prevail. That will not be your experience in CRM 110.

In this class, we will follow the course description by discussing "issues in criminal justice." In the process, different sides of key issues will be presented and critiqued. Please note that whereas political leftists author virtually all of the readings in your other courses, conservatives and libertarians author many of the readings in this course. This is done so that you will be exposed to beliefs that contradict those of the vast majority of your professors. Often, these dissenting views are presented only as caricatures. In this class, you will hear from the proponents of such views directly. If this causes you to encounter viewpoints that bother you or make you feel uncomfortable, that is good. There will be no safe space into which you can retreat. Instead, you will be required to take off your intellectual training wheels—something that should have happened for the first time in grade school, rather than in college. This means that you will be expected to express your constitutional right to object to their point of view. In a nutshell, I expect you to act like adults while you are in this classroom. This means that you will refrain from trying to manipulate others by asserting that your emotions are more important than their ideas.

Grading: Five tests will be given. The first four will be book tests designed to determine whether you have read your assigned books carefully. The last one will be comprehensive. I will count four of them. Each will be 25 percent of your grade. This means that if you are satisfied with your grade after the four book tests then you will not need to take the fifth test, which is a comprehensive final. If you do, it will substitute for your lowest book test grade.

DO NOT COME TO SEE ME BEFORE OR AFTER YOUR ABSENCE WITH AN EXPLANATION. I WILL NOT TAKE ROLL IN THIS CLASS. I WILL ALLOW THOSE WHO SHOULD NOT BE IN COLLEGE TO WEED THEMSELVES OUT OF THE STUDENT POPULATION BY SKIPPING AND FAILING.

Course Outline: This course will be broken down into fifteen sections. The reading assignments and major questions or topics to be addressed in each section are as follows:

SECTION 1
How do we approach criminal justice policy in America?
The distinction between liberal and conservative approaches to crime causation and control will be discussed. We need to understand why liberals agree with other liberals, why

conservatives agree with other conservatives, and why the two sides never seem to agree with one another.

Reading: Thomas Sowell (optional).

SECTION 2
What happened to the criminal law when Roe v. Wade was decided—and, perhaps more importantly, what will happen if it is overturned? We first need to talk about what *Roe* said and what it did not say. Next, we will talk about the very real prospect that it could be overturned—and who could be subject to criminal liability if that happens.

Movie: *Unplanned* (optional).

SECTION 3
How do we measure crime in order to assess the efficacy of popular gun control measures? We often hear that gun control measures have been tried and tested and have succeeded in other nations. But how did we arrive at that conclusion? And, furthermore, does any existing evidence contradict that conclusion?

Reading: Lott (optional).

SECTION 4
Is there any theoretical basis for believing that arming citizens can actually reduce crime? If the answer to this question is "yes" then what other crime control measures are called for among citizens who disagree or do not wish to exercise their right to bear arms?

Reading: Felson (optional).

SECTION 5

What are the differences between the truly insane and the totally depraved that would justify absolving the former of criminal liability? As we look at the killing of Kitty Genovese, also recall our discussion of routine activities theory. What could have prevented her rape and murder? What could she have done, if anything? What could others have done, if anything? What could politicians have done, if anything?

Reading: Cook (required). Test one.

SECTION 6

Should we further limit the death penalty or just eliminate it altogether? We will think long and hard about the consequences of allowing Kitty Genovese's killer to live. But we will also consider some related questions. What if she had survived the attack? Would there have been a compelling case for executing her rapist? And what if her killer had been mentally handicapped rather than psychopathic? What difference does that make and what difference should that make in our moral calculus?

SECTION 7

Who has won the battle over the Supreme Court? The political left is concerned that the republic will be lost if the current balance on the Supreme Court continues to shift. But haven't they already won the battle in many respects? What do they have left to accomplish? What is left for conservatives to conserve?

Readings: Lee (required) and Levin (optional). Test two.

SECTION 8

What are the major progressive theories of crime? Perhaps the more important questions are a) why these theories have been such a failure and b) why academics won't admit it. I'll answer them both.

Movie: *Boyz in the Hood* (required).

SECTION 9

What does the evidence say about the claims of the Black Lives Matter movement? More importantly, is it possible that misrepresenting the nature of white cop on black suspect violence ultimately increases intra-racial crime? That would seem to be a strange claim. But is there something to the idea of the so-called Ferguson effect? If so, do criminologists bear any responsibility for misrepresenting social problems for ideological reasons—and thus possibly exacerbating them?

Reading: McDonald (required). Test three.

SECTION 10

Is the criminal justice system really systematically racist? Here, we will critique the existing research in the field of criminology. Are these studies really scientific? Or are the studies themselves systematically rigged in order to produce a result that creates problems for tenured intellectuals to solve?

Reading: Wilbanks (optional).

SECTION 11

Is there really a rape epidemic on our college campuses? How could rape be going down in the society at large while simultaneously increasing on college campuses—

moreover, by about 50 percent in the last five years of the Obama presidency? And why have we seen a sudden series of successful suits against universities that have apparently railroaded innocent students through campus rape tribunals? Finally, why do universities conduct their own rape trials in the first place?

Reading: Johnson and Taylor (required). Test four.

SECTION 12

What was that you were saying about white privilege? There was a time when it was simply understood that it is always indecent to denigrate people (especially in public) because of their race. Today, people are routinely told in public settings (e.g., college classrooms) that their point of view is to be discounted because it is a function of a racial privilege, which must be "checked." This is often a crude way of saying that their point of view needs to be excluded from the marketplace of ideas.

Originally, a domestic terrorist group called the Weather Underground launched the war on white privilege in the 1960s. Now, the ideology of these terrorists is mainstream in academia. And that has had dangerous consequences on many campuses.

Enter the Duke Lacrosse case. As we examine the Duke debacle, note that the disturbing trends we saw during the Obama administration (see section 11) were already in place well before he was elected. In other words, we cannot simply blame our forty-fourth president.

Reading: Taylor and Johnson (optional).

SECTION 13

What was that you were saying about patriarchal oppression? Feminist professors often talk about oppression. But you don't see many of them boarding leaky boats and paddling their way toward Cuba in order to escape patriarchy and achieve gender equality. Women have it good in America. This is especially true of married women.

Here, we step back from theory and examine the reality of sexism and the law by taking a brief look at what routinely goes on in family court in America. Specifically, we will examine what happens to men accused of crimes in the midst of divorce and custody proceedings. Students will be asked how common family law practices can possibly be squared with the constitution—particularly the Fourteenth Amendment (Hint: They cannot).

Reading: Baskerville (optional).

SECTION 14
How does the media distort your view of crime and justice? There are thousands of examples we could use but we will stick with two: Matthew Shepard and Columbine. To call the coverage of these two cases "fake news" is to understate the matter. These cases are examples of media malpractice. As you think about these cases and others, what are the common themes in media representations of crime and justice?

Reading: Cullen (optional), Jimenez (optional).

SECTION 15
What is the future of the Supreme Court? We began this course by talking about differences between conservatives (who sometimes want to minimize due process to control crime) and liberals (who sometimes want to allow more

crime to maximize due process and thus protect the innocent from wrongful conviction). But what has happened in recent years to liberal support for due process?

Also, how will a toxic political environment in Washington D.C. affect an increasingly politicized Supreme Court. Our emphasis in the final section will be on the Kavanaugh confirmation hearings and what they say about the stability of our republic.

Reading: Hemingway (optional).

Student Learning Objectives:

1. Students will learn that "student learning objectives" are meaningless requirements imposed on professors by bureaucrats. Thus, students should generally ignore them.
2. Students will begin to recognize for the first time that their education is not complete when they graduate from college. In fact, it is never complete. Much like criminal justice, education is a process, rather than a result.

And every syllabus ends with this:

Who is Davidson Myers?

If you have not yet heard (or read) about me, I am an outspoken professor who has, at times, been critical of certain aspects of evolution. I mention this because it affects the way I see you and the way I will treat you this semester.

Rather than seeing you as the mere product of random mutation, I see you as a unique individual endowed by his Creator—not just with a right to life, liberty, and the pursuit of happiness—but with a purpose. Each one of you has unique and special talents and along with that a distinct purpose in life that makes you not just unique but irreplaceable.

Unfortunately, I sometimes have students who resist fulfilling their God-given potential. Often, they do things in college that hurt their chances of success in life. One good example is a fellow named Davidson Myers whom I first taught in the fall of 1999.

Davidson, who aspired to be a lawyer, came into my class late on several occasions. He was also prone to turning around in his seat and yapping in class with another student by the name of Paula Tyndall. This went on for weeks until Davidson the aspiring lawyer got back his first test grade. It was a "C" in a class called "Criminal Law and Procedure" that was central to his career aspirations. He was devastated so he came by the office to see me.

When Davidson came by, he told me he could not afford to be getting "Cs" because he was going to be a lawyer. My response to Davidson was simple: "No, you're never going to be a lawyer. Not until you get your (offensive term deleted) together."

A truly bizarre thing happened to Davidson after I told him to get to class on time and pay attention or he would never amount to anything. He actually did what I told him to do.

In addition to getting an "A" on my next exam he took another of my courses the next semester. He got an "A." Today, he is a lawyer married to another lawyer. He and his wife have successful practices here in North Carolina. When I called him to ask permission to share his story he laughed uncontrollably. I consider him a friend and someone I would hire were I to get into trouble with the law.

By the way, here is the (threefold) reason I am sharing Davidson's story with you today:

1. Every time you enter my class late—even one second late (as you should be in your chair before the class begins)—I will send you an email with the question "Who is Davidson Myers?" in the subject line. If you can tell me who he is, I will only deduct one point from your final average. If you cannot, I will send another email, which will cost another point.

2. Every time you flap your jaws with one of your classmates while I am lecturing, I will send you an email with the question "Who is Davidson Myers?" in the subject line. If you can tell me who he is, I will only deduct one point from your final average. If you cannot, I will send another email, which will cost another point.

3. Every time I see or hear your cell phone in my class, I will send you an email with the question "Who is Davidson Myers?" in the subject line. If you can tell me who he is, I will only deduct one point from your final average. If you cannot, I will send another email, which will cost another point.

All points deducted will go into a special fund available to credit (at semester's end) those students who follow the rules. In other words, they will go to those who never received a "Who is Davidson Myers?" email.

Mike teaching at Summit Ministries in Manitou Springs, Colorado, which he did for his last twelve consecutive summers. (Photos courtesy of Summit Ministries)

CHAPTER 13

Teaching to the Ten

Originally published in 2014.

The syllabi showed you what Mike taught, but Mike's genius was how he taught it, how he interacted with the students. Mike had substance as well as style. He was tough but fair, funny, caring, involved, and popular. These next few chapters should provide some insight into both his personality and his pedagogy.

Dear CRM 381 Students:

Welcome back! I just wanted to write and let you know that the syllabus is up and running on the departmental web page. I have been instructed to direct you to the link rather than distribute individual copies. The university needs to save money on paper so the LGBTQIA Office can continue to offer orgasm awareness seminars and so the Women's Resource Center can continue to promote abortion.

In addition to going over the syllabus on day one, I plan to introduce each one of you to my somewhat informal teaching philosophy. Actually, this will be the first time I ever make a statement of teaching philosophy, despite the fact that it is my twenty-first year to teach here at UNC-Wilmington. In a nutshell, that philosophy can be summarized in the phrase "twenty-seventy-ten."

When it comes to students, there are at least three distinct groups. They follow in order from the least pleasant to the most pleasant among you.

1. The Tweeny Twenty.
2. The Sagacious Seventy.
3. The Tenacious Ten.

The first group, the Tweeny Twenty, derives its name from its character and its proportions. This is the group of students who, as the name implies, are woefully immature, to almost preadolescent proportions. Fortunately, they are only a minority—about 20 percent of the student population.

The Tweeny Twenty somehow managed to get out of high school without having even a vague sense of what they want to accomplish in life. But they are able to go to college for a few years to explore their options because a) anyone can get into college these days, and b) anyone can get a government-backed loan to help pay for college these days. And so, they go. What else is there to do?

Having no clue what they are doing in college, they behave as clueless individuals do. They come and go from class as they please—arriving late and leaving early. They dress inappropriately as if they are coming from a bar or are heading to the beach. In short, they come to college for social reasons. To party. To meet a spouse. Or maybe to meet a "connection" or someone who will "hook them up" with a job upon graduation.

I will do everything within my ability to drive these people out of the classroom before the drop date. That is my sincere promise to the other 80 percent of you.

The second group, the Sagacious Seventy, also derives its name from its character and its proportions. This is the group of students who, as the name implies, are shrewder and more goal-oriented than the Tweeny Twenty. Fortunately—I only say "fortunately" because they are fairly well behaved and manageable—they are about 70 percent of the student population.

Having some clue of what they are doing in college, they behave as rational individuals. They come to class pretty regularly and go through the motions in order to get their course credit. They have calculated that having a degree is better than not having a degree and that the amount they pay in student loans will be exceeded by the salary increase that accompanies having a college degree. Of course, many of these students have miscalculated and will never pay off their loans, but that is another issue to be explored at a later date.

In short, these students come to college to get credentialed. They know that employers want to see an applicant's degree, because that means they had the stick-to-it-ness to set a goal and follow through. They also know that it doesn't require much work to get their expensive degree, so they divert study time toward work time. They take a part-time job in order to keep their student loans down even if this means turning in sub-par work. They know their professors have come to expect sub-par work. Like most of our students, they are intelligent and keenly self-interested. They do the cost-benefit analysis and make a reasonable decision in a difficult situation that is becoming more difficult as college becomes more expensive.

I will do everything within my ability to threaten these people into doing work that is only slightly sub-par, instead of clearly deficient. I know they are used to being given good grades for work that is clearly deficient. But I also know that they cannot risk failing my class. So, I will threaten them and hopefully (through fear) motivate them to soar towards mediocrity in their academic work output. It's really the best I can hope for in an age of hyper-inflated hire (misspelling intentional) education.

The last group, the Tenacious Ten, also derives its name from its character and its proportions. This is the group of students who, as the name implies, are highly determined and persistent and cannot easily be distracted from their goals. Unfortunately, they are only about 10 percent of the student population.

The Tenacious Ten may well have good genes. I don't know for sure. But I do know that they usually had good parents who taught them good life lessons. Also, more than likely, they had good counselors in their schools or in the churches. And so, they are focused and ready from day one.

In short, the Tenacious Ten are here because they desire specific knowledge that will help them attain a specific goal. As a result, they have an intrinsic appreciation of the material I plan to teach throughout the semester. So, there is no need to threaten or cajole or manipulate them into performing at expected levels. They just do it because they come to college having already gotten into the habit of doing it on their own.

This message is just my way of reminding you that when I talk about "our" class I am not talking about all thirty of you. I am talking to about three of you: those who constitute the Tenacious Ten percent. You are the only reason I am still teaching. I look forward to finding out who you are. I don't suspect it will take very long to identify you.

I hope this message finds you well. If you are in the Tweeny Twenty, I hope it scares the hell out of you—so much so that you drop the course. Otherwise, I will see you in class on Monday.

Mike had commented multiple times about the decline in the quality of incoming students since he wrote this in 2014. If I were able to ask him for an update, I wonder: Would the Tweeny Twenty now be the Dirty Thirty? Or perhaps even the Forlorn Forty?

Despite his growing frustration with the decline in student quality, I know that he never lost his love for "Teaching to the Ten." For example, on 09/10/2019, he posted the following:

After a great evening in "Trials of the Century," I return home with the satisfaction of knowing that I was born to do what I do for a living. Nothing is as satisfying as knowing your life is not wasted by not following your calling.

Mike certainly followed his calling, and his life was well lived indeed.

We do not have any video of Mike teaching at UNCW, but here is a short video of Mike teaching at Summit in Colorado in the summer:

https://www.youtube.com/ watch?v=xtKG-tT0Y2c&ab_channel=TonyEvans

Below are a few samples of what Mike's students thought about his personality and pedagogy:

2. (I would)/would not recommend this instructor to other students because . . .
He is very caring and sweet. He influences students to be interested.

3. This instructor (does)/does not show respect for students as evidenced by . . . allowing them to express their opinions and encouraging everyone to participate.

4. Classroom presentations of this instructor are . . . very well thought out and prepared for each class.

I would/would not recommend this instructor to other students because . . .
he cares about the students, tries his best to get the most out of them, to motivate them

5. I (would)/would not recommend this instructor to other students because . . .
he is a great person

This instructor does/does not show respect for students as evidenced by . . .
He shows a great deal of respect for the students & I admire that in a professor.

Classroom presentations of this instructor are . . .
Great! He makes class very interesting w/ personal stories & his sarcastic comments.

Classroom presentations of this instructor are . . .
groovy

3. This instructor (does)/does not show respect for students as evidenced by . . . his deep interest in his students and his need of being able to relate to each and everyone

3. This instructor (does)/does not show respect for students as evidenced by . . . allowing us to have our own opinion and views.

CHAPTER 14

Innovative Grading Policies

In this chapter, we again deviate somewhat from the usual format of this book and combine two articles in one chapter, as they complement each other very well indeed. These show how Mike used humor and satire to drive home his points. (Although, in his public life, this would be his downfall because so many of his critics are humorless and do not understand satire.)

My New Spread the Wealth Grading Policy

Originally published in 2009; updated and sent to students in 2019.

Good afternoon, students! I'm writing you this email to announce that I'm making some changes in the grading policies I announced previously in our course syllabus. As you know, this is an election year, and we again have an opportunity to elect a new president. After seeing several of you with "Bernie 2020" and "Feel the Bern" bumper stickers on your laptops, I thought it would be nice to align our class policies with the policies you seem to be aligning yourself with by supporting an openly socialist candidate.

Previously, I announced that I would use a ten-point grading scale, which means that 90 percent of one hundred is an "A," 80 percent is a "B," 70 percent is a "C," and 60 percent is enough for a passing grade of "D."

The new policy I am announcing today is that those who score above ninety on the first exam will have points deducted and given to students at the bottom of the grade distribution. For example, if a student gets a ninety-nine, I will then deduct nine points and give them to the person with the lowest grade. If a person scores ninety-five, I will then deduct five points and give them to the person with the second lowest grade. If someone scores ninety-three, I will then deduct three points and give them to the next lowest person. And so on.

My point, rather obviously, is that any points above ninety are really not needed since you have an "A" regardless of whether you score ninety or ninety-nine. Nor am I convinced that you need to save those points for a rainy day. Those who are failing need the points.

After our second examination, I intend to take a more complex approach to the practice of grade redistribution. I will not be looking at your second test scores but, instead, at the average of your first two test scores. In the process, I may well decide to start taking some points from students in the "B" range. For example, if someone has an average of eighty-five after two tests, I may take a few points and give them away to someone who is failing or who is in danger of failing. I think this is fair because the person with an eighty-five average is probably unlikely to climb up to an "A" or fall down to a "C." I may be wrong in some individual cases, but, of course, my principal concern is not the individual. I care more about the collective.

By the end of the semester, I will abandon any formal guidelines and just redistribute points in a way that seems just, or fair, to me. I will not rely upon any standards other than my very strong and passionate feelings concerning social justice. In the process, I will not merely seek to eliminate inequality. I will also seek to eliminate the possibility of failure.

I know some are concerned that my system may impact their lives in a very profound way. Grade redistribution will undoubtedly cause some grade point average redistribution. And this, in turn, will mean that some people will not get into the law school or medical school of their choice. Or maybe someday you will be represented by a lawyer—or operated on by a doctor—who is not of the highest quality.

These are all, of course, legitimate long-term concerns. But I believe we need to remain focused on the short term.

My New Life Difficulty Grading Scale

Originally published in 2004.

Dear Fall 2004 students:

First of all, let me apologize for writing to you so late in the year after so many of you have gone home for the semester. Most of you thought that the semester was over and that grades had been finalized, so you didn't expect to get this mass email. But, nonetheless, I urge you to read this message carefully. It may mean a change in your grade for the semester that we just finished together.

I am writing to you because a student recently contacted me to question her final grade in my class. First, she wanted me to explain our complex grading system. As you know, this involves adding your three test scores together and dividing by three. Fortunately, I was able to convince her that there had been no computational errors so we could move on to the issue that was really bothering her. She had had a 'rough' semester and wanted me to give her some 'consideration' for the difficulties she had encountered, which, according to her, adversely affected her performance in my class.

In addition to breaking up with her boyfriend, this concerned student was having difficulty paying her bills and had to work thirty hours a week while taking fifteen credit hours last semester. These difficulties added up, in her opinion, to at least a one letter grade drop in her class performance.

It may come as a surprise to all of you but, after listening to her hardship story, I have decided to change this student's grade. Specifically, I plan to raise it one letter grade in order to give her the outcome she would have earned if life had gone as she expected it to, without any unforeseen difficulties.

I came to this decision based upon two principal factors. First, there was the sheer sincerity of the student's argument. She really felt that she deserved a better grade. I know that should have been enough, but the second factor was the real clincher. When she left my office and went to her car (which was parked in the faculty parking lot with a $25 ticket on the windshield) I noticed that it was a $30,000 SUV. How can the student afford a $30,000 gas-guzzling SUV if her studies are interfering with her work schedule? And those $25 parking tickets really add up after a while. Clearly, something has to give.

After I committed to raising this student's grade, it occurred to me that I should probably contact all of you to see how your semester went. And, in fairness, if any of you experienced any unexpected difficulties, you should have the right to enumerate them and explain exactly how much they hurt your performance in class last semester. Using the university honor system, I will take you at your word and adjust your grades accordingly.

The difficult part will be applying this policy retroactively. In order to be completely fair, I will have to go back and adjust the grades of everyone who has presented me with a life difficulty claim over the last twenty-three semesters. I have provided a few examples of the cases I can recall, hoping that the enumeration of these cases will give you an idea of the kinds of benefits to which you might be entitled.

In 1993, one of my students experienced the death of two of his maternal grandmothers within the course of a month. Accordingly, students will be given one letter grade for each family death, whether it occurs in the nuclear or extended family.

In 1996, a student asked to be exempt from the class attendance policy because her recent absences were caused by the unexpected outbreak of a venereal disease. Accordingly, students will be given one letter grade for each STD contracted during the semester.

In 1999, a student missed a month of class after getting pregnant and then having an abortion between the second and third exam. She wanted special consideration because the father of the child had not been sufficiently supportive. Accordingly, students getting pregnant out of wedlock will be given one letter grade for each unexpected pregnancy. An additional letter grade will be given for actually aborting the unborn child.

In 2001, a black student told me that she needed to spend time at the African American Center every day in order to 'get the support she needs to make it through the day.' Not wanting to be accused of racism, I declined to suggest that she spend the time in the library studying to improve her grades. In the future, students will be awarded one letter grade for taking classes while being black.

In 2002, a lesbian student came by the office to let me know that, after a rough semester, she was switching back to heterosexuality. Being gay or lesbian on a college campus is tough enough to earn a one-letter grade adjustment. Being unsure of your sexual orientation (or your gender) will earn you a two-letter grade bonus.

Students reading the above cases should not be led to believe that they have read an exhaustive list. As a conservative white male Protestant heterosexual, I am careful not to impose my own reality upon those who do not share my privilege. Thus, you may feel free to argue other circumstances I have not have previously considered. As always, the focus should be upon your feelings.

As controversial as it may seem, my new life difficulty grading scale will help us to achieve a goal that should make all of us feel comfortable. That goal is nothing less than the destruction of the antiquated notion that people should work to overcome life's difficulties with no advanced guarantee of the outcome they desire.

By the way, here is what Mike's Department Chair wrote in his 1997 Annual Evaluation:

"Dr. Adams was clearly a gifted and accomplished teacher who was eagerly sought after as an academic advisor. All

indications are that he was a productive and talented scholar and a responsible university and departmental citizen."

And in his 2001 Annual Evaluation:

"Dr. Adams is a skilled, passionate, and dedicated teacher, productive and enthusiastic scholar, and good departmental and university citizen. He continues to demonstrate that he is one of the best instructors in our department and in the university."

Mike displayed this framed First Amendment prominently in his office over his desk. It is one of the few things he had on his office wall, since there was little available wall space thanks to wall-to-wall and floor-to-ceiling bookcases filled with books.

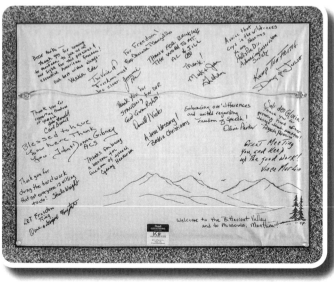

CHAPTER 15

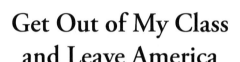

Get Out of My Class
and Leave America

Originally published in 2015.

This was included in Townhall's "Year in Review: The 15 Most Popular Stories of 2015." Mike said it surpassed one million shares on Facebook.

Author's Note: The following column is comprised of excerpts taken from my first lectures on the first day of classes this semester at UNC-Wilmington. I reproduced these remarks with the hope that they would be useful to other professors teaching at public universities all across America. Feel free to use this material if you already have tenure.

Welcome back to class, students! I am Mike Adams your criminology professor here at UNC-Wilmington. Before we get started with the course, I need to address an issue that is causing problems here at UNCW and in higher education all across the country. I am talking about the growing minority of students who believe they have a right to be free from being offended. If we don't reverse this dangerous trend in our society, there will soon be a majority of young people who will need to walk around in plastic bubble suits to protect them in the event that they come into contact with a dissenting viewpoint. That mentality is unworthy of an American.

Let's get something straight right now. You have no right to be unoffended. You have a right to be offended with regularity. It is the price you pay for living in a free society. If you don't understand that, you are confused and dangerously so. In part, I blame your high school teachers for failing to teach you basic civics before you got your diploma. Most of you went to public high schools, which are a disaster. Don't tell me that offended you. I went to a public high school.

Of course, your high school might not be the problem. It is entirely possible that the main reason why so many of you are confused about free speech is that piece of paper hanging on the wall right over there. Please turn your attention to that ridiculous document that is framed and hanging by the door. In fact, take a few minutes to read it before you leave class today. It is our campus speech code. It specifically says that there is a requirement that everyone must only engage in discourse that is "respectful." That assertion is as ludicrous as it is illegal. I plan to have that thing ripped down from every classroom on campus before I retire.

One of my grandfathers served in World War I. My step-grandfather served in World War II. My sixth great grandfather enlisted in the American Revolution when he was only thirteen. These great men did not fight so we could simply relinquish our rights to the enemy within our borders. That enemy is the Marxists who run our public universities. If you are a Marxist and I just offended you, well, that's tough. I guess they don't make communists like they used to.

Of course, this ban on "disrespectful" speech is really only illusory. The university that created these speech restrictions then turns around and sponsors plays like *The Vagina Monologues,* which is loaded with profanity, including the c-word—the most offensive and disrespectful word a person could ever possibly apply to a woman. It is pure, unadulterated hypocrisy.

So, the university position can be roughly summarized as follows: Public university administrators have a First Amendment right to use disrespectful profanity, but public university students do not. This turns the First Amendment on its head. The university has its free speech analysis completely backwards. And that's why they need to be sued.

Before we go, let us take a few minutes to look at the last page of your syllabus where I explain the importance of coming to class on time, turning off your cell phone, and refraining from talking during lectures. In that section, I explain that each of you has God-given talents and that your Creator endowed you with a purpose in life that is thwarted when you develop these bad habits.

Unbelievably, a student once complained to the Department chairwoman that my mention of God and a Creator was a violation of Separation of Church and State. Let me be as clear as I possibly can: If any of you actually think that my decision to paraphrase the Declaration of Independence in the course syllabus is unconstitutional, then you suffer from severe intellectual hernia.

Indeed, it takes hard work to become stupid enough to think that the Declaration of Independence is unconstitutional. If you agree with the student who made that complaint, then you are probably just an anti-religious zealot. Therefore, I am going to ask you to do exactly three things and do them in the exact order that I specify.

First, get out of my class. You can fill out the drop slip over at James Hall. Just tell them you don't believe in true diversity, and you want to be surrounded by people who agree with your twisted interpretation of the constitution, simply because they are the kind of people who will protect you from having your beliefs challenged or your feelings hurt.

Second, withdraw from the university. If you find that you are actually relieved because you will no longer be in a class where your beliefs might be challenged, then you aren't ready for college. Go get a job building houses so you can work with some illegal aliens who will help you gain a better appreciation of what this country has to offer.

Finally, if this doesn't work, then I would simply ask you to get the hell out of the country. The ever-growing thin-skinned minority you have joined is simply ruining life in this once-great nation. Please move to some place like Cuba where you can enjoy the company of communists and get excellent health care. Just hop on a leaky boat and start paddling your way towards utopia. You will not be missed.

Thank you for your time. I'll see most of you when classes resume on Monday.

It is tragic that Mike's enemies did not realize that Mike was also fighting for THEIR freedom of speech, not just his. If you are only fighting for your speech, then you are not truly fighting for freedom of speech—as Mike was. Here are some other Mike Adams quotes related to freedom of speech:

The constitution only protects offensive speech. If it only protected inoffensive speech, then it would be useless. That which is not offensive is not in need of protection.

Our constitution protects offensive speech. It doesn't protect offended individuals.

Censorship is bullying.

If my columns make you feel uncomfortable, the solution is for you to stop reading, not for me to stop writing.

A UNCW feminist claims I should not be allowed to speak at UNCW because my past speech has made people at UNCW mad. Imagine a country where people are only allowed to speak if they have never made someone mad. Imagine further a country where people merely have to pretend to be angry in order to permanently silence people with opposing views.

[This was written years ago. Today, we no longer have to imagine. Sadly, as usual, his prediction came true—and he became one of those who were permanently silenced.]

I'm so old, I can remember when Democrats supported free speech.

I recoil whenever I hear people use terms like "homophobe," "Islamophobe," or "xenophobe." If someone disagrees with you on same-sex marriage, foreign policy, or immigration, it does ot mean they are driven by an irrational fear. It just means they have a contrary opinion. Characterizing dissent as mental illness is a dangerous step in the direction of totalitarianism.

Photo courtesy of Summit Ministries.

Photo courtesy of Kevin Yi.

CHAPTER 16

UNC-Wilmington Feminists
Abort Free Speech

Originally published in 2002.

In his twenty-seven years as a UNCW professor, Mike taught several thousand students in the classroom. In his twelve summers at Summit Ministries, it is estimated that he spoke to 15,000 students. In his seventeen years as a columnist, he extended his reach beyond the classroom to hundreds of thousands of readers.

This early column was not his first, but it is significant because it was so well-received that it helped him get hired by Townhall in 2003. He would go on to write approximately 1,200 columns for them, Daily Wire, and others before he passed.

The UNCW administration's hatred of Mike's columns ultimately resulted in the court case we will read about in the next chapter.

When a new Women's Resource Center was established at my university (UNC-Wilmington), I was concerned that it would serve as more of a resource for feminist professors than for female students. I also suspected that the center would try to advance a "pro-choice" agenda with little tolerance for the views of pro-life advocates.

Those suspicions were confirmed during my recent visit to the center's web site. I noticed that the center claimed a dedication to education and advocacy on a variety of issues facing women of "all backgrounds, beliefs, and orientations." It also claimed an interest in working with many community-based organizations and in maintaining "clear lines of communication" between the students and "any organizations involved." Despite all that, the site gives contact information for the "pro-choice" Planned Parenthood, while Life Line, a "pro-life" center, is conspicuously not mentioned.

I contacted the site's manager with a simple request for the center to add Life Line's contact information near that of Planned Parenthood, and I was directed to Dr. Kathleen Berkeley. Berkeley had pushed for the establishment of the Women's Resource Center and is in charge of the Center until its first official director assumes her duties in July. After a few days of deliberation and meeting with the dean, Berkeley denied my request, stating "the addition of Life Line Pregnancy Center would duplicate information provided by Planned Parenthood."

Of course, there is no "non-duplication requirement" for organizations posting information on the center's web site. For example, the site features two community organizations offering rape crisis counseling—and no reasonable person could object to that kind of "duplication." Surely, if someone built a second domestic violence shelter in town, the center wouldn't deny a request to list it for "duplication." Not only is this supposed "non-duplication" standard non-existent and unworkable, but it is also utterly inapplicable to the case at hand.

The differences between Life Line and Planned Parenthood are far greater than their similarities. The decision to keep Life Line's information away from students is yet another silly episode revealing the fundamental dishonesty of the university's so-called commitment to diversity. It is no accident that the university library has Planned Parenthood's response to Bernard Nathanson's film *The Silent Scream* and a book by Berkeley referring to *The Silent Scream* as "grisly sensationalism"—but not *The Silent Scream* itself. The university appears to prefer students reading reviews offered from one perspective than looking at the original—there's a risk the students might come up with a different opinion.

The problem with higher education today is not that people are unaware that the diversity movement is dishonest. It's that among those people with reasonable objections to the diversity agenda, there are too few willing to do something about it. Administrators at public universities simply have no right to take money from taxpayers and use it to advance their own political causes while systematically suppressing the views of their opponents.

I hope everyone reading this article will "duplicate" my efforts to expand the marketplace of ideas at their local university. If your tax dollars are being used to support a one-sided view on the issue of abortion, respectfully ask for information on the other side to be included. If you are denied, take your case before the court of public opinion or, if necessary, a court of law. After all, the right to free speech is older than the "right to choose." And censorship is decidedly "anti-choice."

Although Mike would write on a broad range of issues, abortion and free speech would remain two of his main topics and would intersect periodically, as they did here. In fact, when he passed away, Mike was working on a manuscript titled Aborting Free Speech, *which has been published posthumously (as I also mentioned at the end of Chapter 9). To gain a better understanding of Mike's take on abortion and free speech (and many other issues), please read his book* Letters to a Young Progressive. *(And then, if you just can't get enough of him, you will likely enjoy his first two books,* Welcome to the Ivory Tower of Babel *and* Feminists Say the Darndest Things.*)*

EXCELLENCE

The Greek Affairs Review & Recognition Committee & The Office of the Dean of Students

on behalf of The University of North Carolina at Wilmington

are proud to recognize

Dr. Mike S. Adams

as

Faculty Member of the Year

_____
Brandi Hephner LaBanc

_____
Dr. Brian O. Hemphill

_____
Dr. Terrance Curran

1999 – 2000 Greek Affairs Review and Recognition Reception – April 18, 2000

We, the members of the jury, find as follows:

I. SUBSTANTIAL OR MOTIVATING FACTOR ELEMENT

Was the plaintiff's speech activity a substantial or motivating factor in the defendants' decision to not promote the plaintiff?

Yes   (Yes or No)

_(NOTE: You will reach the second issue only if you answe~
"Yes" to this first issue. If your verdict is "No," ski[
to the bottom of this page and have the foreperson sign an(
date the verdict form and return to the courtroom.)_

II. AFFIRMATIVE DEFENSE

Would the defendants have reached the same decision not to promote the plaintiff even in the absence of the plaintiff's speech activity?

_NO_   (Yes or No)

SO SAY WE ALL.

3-20-14

_____
Foreperson

Date

CHAPTER 17

Adams v. UNCW

Everything you have read so far has been leading up to a monumental clash between Mike and his university. This was Mike's greatest battle—and his greatest victory.

In spite of his distinguished success as a professor, Mike's views, not surprisingly, were intensely unpopular among his Leftist colleagues. In fact, Mike was bullied for them and denied a promotion. Here is his story, in the transcript of a speech he gave to the Alliance Defending Freedom (ADF) in 2014:

Oh, it is so awesome to be here among friends. I want to begin by telling you guys that I've had some hard decisions to make in my life, but the easiest decision I ever made was to become a plaintiff for the Alliance Defending Freedom back in September of 2006. My journey began as an atheist back in 1993, when I was hired as a professor at UNC-Wilmington, and they loved me back then.

Then, I converted after a prison visit to Ecuador. I was doing some human rights work in 1996, and I converted to theism. After a visit on death row in 1999, doing my work as a criminologist, I went through a study of Christianity and converted to Christianity in the year 2000. Around 2002, I made a decision to start speaking out about the systematic abuses of free speech on college campuses and the tremendous double standards that were going on. I wrote for about four years.

I started writing for the American Family Association's Agape Press, and then I moved on and was hired by townhall. com. And as it came time for me to face that decision, as I went up for promotion to full professor in 2006, I was talking to ADF about the possibility that they might try to retaliate against me for expressing my doubts about their commitment to free expression. We were sort of prepared for this. We got that adverse ruling back on September 15th of 2006 and I demanded a reason.

I received a letter that said I was deficient in every single area: teaching, research, and service. And as I read the letter, I was staring right at my 1998 Professor of The Year Award and looking at my year 2000 Professor of The Year Award that I'd won before I converted to Christianity. And I picked up the phone and there was no question about who I was going to call. I called the Alliance Defending Freedom and made a decision that day that we were going to fight. Easiest decision I ever made in my life. But I had no idea how difficult that road was going to be.

Our case was simply a circumstantial case. They loved me when I was on the other side; then, I converted, and things began to happen. There was some evidence of retaliation, but we began with what was simply a circumstantial case. I really began by applauding the attorneys at the ADF for taking a risky case that was a circumstantial case. We made that decision in 2006. In 2007, on April 10th, we filed in federal court in Greenville, North Carolina. Then, we had to go and beat the obligatory (of course) motion to dismiss from the university because they never admit wrongdoing. They always fight because they're doing it with your tax dollars.

And so, they fought us in the year 2008. And my attorneys had to work very hard in those initial stages. We succeeded and thank God Almighty that that meant that we were able to move into the year 2009 and to move through e-discovery and move into depositions. That took a while because the administration had written 3,000 pages of emails about me. They were sending a lot of emails back and forth, and we began to actually get direct evidence in the case.

People are often confused. I mean, there are Christians out there who don't know if they're in favor of Christian litigation. Well, the problem is that they don't understand the difference between the lost and the Pharisees. Pharisees are false teachers who are teaching untruths and they are fully aware of it. And those are the people who were in charge of our universities.

We were able to get these internal emails before they sat down and met. All of these professors were asked to evaluate me along the lines of teaching and research and service. And they weren't mentioning anything about my academic articles. They were logging on to townhall.com. I am convinced that I know where the term "hate speech" comes from. It's speech that the left hates because they are not intelligent enough to rebut it. That is the problem. It is a projection of their intellectual inadequacies because they went crazy reading these columns. Most normal people just stop reading stuff that they hate, but they were into it.

We were also able to get internal emails that showed that even the Chancellor of the university had tried to change the promotion criteria to add a new category of collegiality, simply because she was angry that I criticized her in a public fashion. And thank God Almighty we found all of that direct evidence. So, what do you think happens when we find all of this direct evidence in 2009? Of course, the other side just immediately gives up, right? Wrong.

What they decided to do, and I don't want to get bogged down in a bunch of legal terminology and talk about Supreme Court precedent and all of that. All the lawyers here know about the Garcetti decision from 2006. The university tried to interpret this Supreme Court decision to suggest that when I wrote columns publicly, that they were fully protected by the First Amendment. But that when I simply mentioned them on my promotion application, suddenly they were transformed into official duties, and they had no First Amendment protection whatsoever.

For years, I'd been accusing them of not supporting the First Amendment and their response in the lawsuit was, "You can't say that." That was my point, right? We were shocked when they made the argument and a very aggressive interpretation of Garcetti v. Ceballos. I think we were even more shocked when, on the 10th of March 2010, Judge Malcolm Howard, in my case, accepted their argument, and he threw the case out of court. Wow, one of the worst days of my life, because when that decision was rendered, that was eight years into my career as a person who was an activist talking about the First Amendment on college campuses. And here I am holding myself out as this expert on campus free speech. And we suffered this crushing defeat.

That afternoon, we got the very bad news that it had been thrown out of court, and by that evening, it was on all of the headlines on the evening news. UNCW Professor Loses Lawsuit Against University. I did not sleep that night, but I got up the next morning at about 9:30 because I have tenure. I got that easily when I was a leftist. But I was up, and

I was doing my morning reading when I received a phone call from a young ADF attorney by the name of Joseph Martins.

Joseph said, "I'm terribly sorry for what happened yesterday. You're a friend of mine and I wish that I could have been the one who broke the news to you. But I want you to know this isn't defeat. This is providence." And I am so glad that was a long-distance phone call because if Martins was in that room, he's bigger than me, but I probably would have punched him.

I thought, "What are you talking about? Suggesting that this was not a defeat, that this was providence?" He said, "Well, ADF hasn't made the decision yet, but I predict that they're going to make the decision to appeal this before the Fourth Circuit Court of Appeals. I think we're going to win. But you know what? If we appeal to the Fourth Circuit and we lose, I'll bet we decide to appeal to the US Supreme Court. And can you imagine what that would be like? All the liberals on the Supreme Court would understand the implications of the decision for academic freedom. Then you'd win. You'd get to go to the Supreme Court."

He said, "No, this isn't a defeat. This is providence." And I began to think one of my lawyers was insane. I was so angry at him. So I go into work that morning, about 11 o'clock because I have tenure, still, somehow. And I showed up there and I thought my career was over. No one wants to hear what Mike Adams has to say about the First Amendment anymore. And all of a sudden, the phone rings and this kid who we will call Tim, because that's his name, calls me from Rhode Island. And he says, "We want you to come to our college to give a speech on the First Amendment."

And I said, "Well, what's the honorarium?" Because I'm capitalist now and everything, I converted. And he told me, and I said, "Oh, absolutely. Yeah, yeah, I'll be there. When is it? Sure, I'll be there." And I said, "What college is this?" He says, "This is Providence College." I said, "Where are you calling from?" He says, "This is Providence." And I said, "Is this Joe?" "No, it's Tim."

So, they hire me. And I thought it was one of these God things, and I decided for the first time, wow, I think everything's going to be okay. And so, we continue. I do nothing, but my attorneys, of course, continue to fight through the year 2010. And they won an opportunity for oral argument on January 26th of 2011. It was fantastic. And it was an incredible thing because we had an opportunity to really see the Associate Attorney General just break down in there. He made this very aggressive position.

We kind of knew going into the argument that two of the appellate judges were on our side, but this Reagan appointee, Niemeyer, did not seem to be on our side. He then begins to throw out hypotheticals and he says, "Well, you're saying that if someone mentioned something on a promotion application, well, they give a speech, it loses First Amendment protection." And he directly asked Tom Ziko, "Could they go and get a copy of the speech and read it and then figure out, no, this guy is pro-life? And because he's pro-life, we can't have him at the rank of full professor?"

The Attorney General would not back down off of that position. And Niemeyer's telling him over and over, "That seems like an awfully aggressive position." In other words, "You better change your argument because I'm trying to help you," but he didn't change. And so, I wasn't surprised at all when, on April 11th, we got that decision from the Fourth Circuit, and it was a unanimous three-to-nothing decision deciding Garcetti does not apply to college professors. It does not apply to academic freedom. And our case was thrown back in court.

Joe Martins had credibility without a doubt, and I began thinking it is providence. He was telling me, this will be a precedent, this will be in the First Amendment law books. And he was correct. The Ninth Circuit has taken up the view since then. It has become an important precedent. But when the university was staring down the barrel and looking at the possibility of a jury trial, at that point, you would think they would settle. In September of 2011, my ADF attorneys were called in for mediation and UNCW made a decision not to try to settle the case. They decided that they were going to insult them personally with extremely, extremely low offers. And I was embarrassed for my university, and I was very sad about what had happened.

They decided to try to file another summary judgment motion. And the judge would rule on it months later and decide once again that their arguments were lacking. And so there we were, facing the possibility of a jury trial and Judge Malcolm Howard decides that he's going to order us to sit down for negotiations again on October 29th, just last year, 2013. And we go, and we're sitting there in a federal courthouse in Wilmington, North Carolina, and they come back again with these insulting offers.

My attorneys have flown in from across the country, doing everything in their ability to settle this thing amicably and acting like Christians, but facing people who believed that they were bulletproof. And we were unable to settle the case. And that's when I realized just the day before my forty-ninth birthday, we're going to trial and Judge Malcolm Howard would in fact set a trial for the 17th of March 2014 and he'd lay it out so that both sides had exactly six hours for opening statements and direct examination and cross examination and closing arguments. It was to be a simple trial, and I thought it should be a simple trial.

It was absolutely amazing, but we filed into that courtroom for a three-day trial, and they got what I thought was a fairly favorable jury. And we finally sat down for an opportunity to go into the heart of the case after jury selection. It would turn into a four-day trial.

And I was so excited the first full day of that trial to have an opportunity to get up in front of a jury of my peers and tell my story and to present the evidence of how, when I was an atheist, I had very high teaching evaluations from the students, and I had high peer evaluations as well. But then suddenly after I converted, my teaching evaluations from the students remained high, but all of a sudden from the faculty, they just began to tank.

And we began to show the list of refereed publications of me versus the people who voted against me. And we simply laid all of the evidence out and we told a story that was true, and that made sense for three hours and it was awesome. And then we went, and we had lunch, and we came back for cross-examination. It was not awesome.

I prefer direct [examination] for the record. I got up on the stand and I sat there for two hours while the Associate Attorney General sat there and just read snippets from my opinion columns. At that point, I'd written 900 columns for townhall.com and they started to pull up statements that they knew were from political satires, they knew were from parodies and they start just presenting these isolated sentences and they have nothing to do with the meaning of the articles. And they played the race card from the bottom of the deck and the gender card as well.

And I remember leaving the courtroom that afternoon and I thought to myself, I apologized to my attorneys. And I said, "We've lost this case." And it's amazing. My attorneys reassured me. And they said, "When we took this case, we'd read your columns. We knew what we were getting into." But I couldn't sleep that evening. I was absolutely convinced that almost seven years to the day after filing the suit, we had lost.

And then all of a sudden it is our chance to cross-examine my department chair, the Marxist department chair, who speaks openly of a revolution in the United States of America, which is funny because they don't have guns, but that's a whole other story. Anyway, her cross-examination only took one hour and was it incredible. My attorneys got up there and decided just to ask her the same questions they had asked her in deposition five years previously, except she forgot to do something before the trial. She forgot to read her deposition and she forgot to prepare. Pride cometh before a fall. And it was ugly. Every time she would say something that contradicted her testimony, Travis Barham, boom, he popped it up on the screen and the jury was glued to the drama. She was caught in a contradiction, which statement is true, this or that. She says both are true. And then she's caught lying about something, and at one point in the cross-examination, she says, "Thanks for reminding me." She's thanking my attorneys as they expose her for committing perjury in a federal trial three times in the course of one hour.

At the end of that testimony, I realized all hope was not lost. I thought we have a chance to win this thing. We go into the final day and my attorney decides to get up there and he's going to give an impassioned defense of the First Amendment. And he gets up there and he talks about how we need a constitution, but a constitution is not enough. We need a bill of rights as well to protect religious liberty, to protect free speech.

And as he is giving this history lesson, and I see this woman sitting on the front row nodding so vigorously, I began to develop a fear that she will fall on the floor in the middle of the courtroom and injure herself. I didn't want to lose her. And he finishes and the jury is charged, and they go out to have lunch and deliberate and they return in 1 hour and 50 minutes. And I see this woman come walking back into the courtroom, holding the envelope. She's the foreperson. Oh my God. I am about to have a cardiac arrest. And I'm a jogger. Wow, it's incredible. And she hands the verdict form off to the clerk and the clerk reads the verdict. And I turned to my attorneys, and I said, "Does that mean we won?" And they said, "Yeah, we won." And the judge said something and banged—I think it was a gavel. I didn't know what was going on.

But all of a sudden, I see this procession of tech supporters, three attorney generals, three council members for the university and a row of defendants because we beat them all on all counts. The Chair, the former Chair, the Dean, the Chancellor and the Board of Trustees. They go walking out of that room and they don't know what has hit them. And, my goodness, that drive home was excellent. I slept so well that night and I slept very well the next night.

And I got in my car, and I drove home, two and a half hours to Wilmington, North Carolina, after spending a week in a hotel room fighting this epic First Amendment battle. And it was at that point that I realized what we were in this for. It's to set an example for young people who are walking into the lion's den. That's what it's about. We teach by our actions. We teach by doing.

A couple of weeks later, Judge Malcolm Howard orders the university to promote me to the highest rank of full professor and orders the university to pay me $50,000 in back pay. Amazingly, one of the most fantastic things about this was that the university that didn't settle was ordered to write a check to the Alliance Defending Freedom for $710,000 in legal fees. Wow. That is a lot of ammunition, ladies and gentlemen, to sue the Pharisees in higher education.

After I rested for a couple of weeks—to be serious, I was completely exhausted—I got an invitation to speak in North Raleigh, North Carolina, at a Baptist Church. I went and I gave a speech on the trial and when it was over, I was walking out of the church and the most incredible thing happened. This elderly black man grabs me by the arm. And he looks at me and he says, "I just want to thank you for that thing that you done for our people." And it really caught me off guard because I said, "My goodness."

This is a man who lived through segregation. And one of the few people in this country who realizes that we are all involved, black and white, in an epic civil rights struggle in the United States of America. It's what he meant. And I responded to him by just what I always do when people try and compliment me on what I've done. I said, "Well, you don't understand, the Lord's been raising me up to do this thing since 1993." And that elderly black man looked at me and he stuck his finger in my face. And he says, "No." He said, "The Lord been raising you up to do this thing since you was a little boy." And he turned and he walked off.

Wow. And it put things into perspective because your battles are going to be epic. Your struggles are going to be great. But let me tell you something. You're here for a reason. You're not here by chance. You're here because the Lord has been raising you up to do something great since you were little boys and little girls. And this is not chance—this is providence.

PART 3

Reflecting

Mike strumming his guitar, 1991. Photo credit: Sally Akers Joachim.

CHAPTER 18

Your Time Is Gonna Come

Originally published in 2011 as "Life and How to Live It, Part XI."

By the way, "Life and How to Live It" is the name of a song by R.E.M. from their 1985 album Fables of the Reconstruction *(which I am listening to as I write these words) and was the namesake for the series of articles that were my primary inspiration for this book.*

I mentioned at the beginning of this book that R.E.M. was one of Mike's favorite acts when he was in college. And it was Mike (with the help of my good friend Ken Carter) who turned me on to them. Which is ironic because, as his older brother, initially, I was one of Mike's musical influences. I later learned that when I was not home, in the mid-seventies, Mike would go into my room and listen to my records. At that time, I would have been annoyed. Now, in my grief, I cling to these fragments. But I digress…

One night during the summer of 1989, I was over at my friend Del Rendon's house. We both lived in Starkville, Mississippi. We also both played guitar. After playing half the songs in the Led Zeppelin acoustic catalog, we started to talk. Del tried to convince me to start playing music for a living with my friend Shannon, who is an enormously talented vocalist. Shannon was also over at Del's house that night, so we both heard an earful of compliments from our kind and humble friend.

By the middle of the summer of 1990, Shannon and I were both making ends meet playing in the local bars. The bar we played in the most was the Bully III in Starkville, where Del waited tables working for our mutual friend David Lee Odom. It took a lot of convincing but one night Del got up on stage with David and sang an old Zeppelin song. The crowd went wild. Then, Del stayed on stage and sang a song he wrote called "Brainstorming." It was and still is my favorite Del Rendon original.

Eventually, it was my turn to encourage Del the way he had once encouraged me. In 1993, I had finally achieved my goal of getting a Ph.D. and landing a job as a professor. Before I left town, I told Del to pick up where we left off. Starkville has a long and proud tradition of great local music. It also has a tight community of musicians who really look out for each other. Jim Beaty, Bill Cooke, Jeff Cummings, Jeffrey Rupp, the list goes on. I'll never forget those guys who have dedicated their lives to making people smile with their talent, their love of music, and their love of the people they play for.

I'm not sure I can really describe the happiness I experienced when I came rolling into Starkville one weekend in 1996, as I drove past the old Bully III and saw Del's name on the marquee. After I turned the car around and found a parking space, I slipped into a seat at a table in the back of the bar. Within just a few minutes, Del recognized me. He called me up to the stage to play an old tune (Zeppelin, of course) called "Your Time Is Gonna Come." It was a great time, and it was great to see Del playing guitar and singing in front of a live audience, without a hint of the old shyness that used to keep him off stage.

When I came back to Starkville in 2000, I met an old girlfriend in one of the old dives I used to play in. When Del's name came up, she started to rave about his new band called Del Rendon and the Puerto Rican Rum Drunks. Before she was finished, none other than Del Rendon came walking into the crowded bar. After we caught up for a few minutes, Del went out to his car to get me a present. It was a copy of *Chameleon*, his band's new CD. In typical Del Rendon fashion, he would not allow me to pay him for it. So, I bought him a beer instead.

I didn't see Del again until 2004. I was doing a book signing in the MSU bookstore after a home football game. Del was playing at a local restaurant/bar called The Veranda. So, I went to see him play. As usual, he called me up to the stage just a few minutes after I walked in the bar. We played a few songs and then ended where we began—with an old Zeppelin tune. "Your Time is Gonna Come" was an appropriate finale. When we finished the song, he just turned to me and thanked me for playing with him. That was the last time I saw Del Rendon alive.

When I picked up the phone that afternoon in the late summer of 2005, I just knew something was wrong. It was Dave Odom. He called to tell me that Del had died just a few hours before. It was the kind of sudden death so many musicians had died before him. But Del was so much more than just another musician.

Del the art teacher would be missed by his students. Del the singer/songwriter would be missed by his fans. Del the friend would be missed by his friends. His family, especially his wife and soulmate, would all be left with big holes in their hearts. They would be more like craters that no one else could ever fill.

Not long after Del passed, I started thinking about God's first great commandment. He said we are supposed to love Him with all of our hearts and all of our souls and all our minds. And that means we have no right to keep the gifts He gave us to ourselves. And, of course, His second great commandment says we are to love our neighbors as ourselves. And that means we must shower them with encouragement when they are doing less with God's gifts than they should be.

The arrow between God's two great commandments points in both directions. When we encourage others to use their God-given talents to make others happy, we do more than just pave the way for the happiness of others. We also pave the way for our own happiness. Those who show kindness and humility are not only the ones most likely to give encouragement. They are also its most likely recipients.

Among the best lessons Del Rendon the teacher taught us is that there's no time to be discouraged. We have to dedicate our lives to encouraging others. Pretty soon, our time is coming, too.

This chapter breaks my heart. If Mike wrote "there's no time to be discouraged," then how did he end up that way? Because even the encouragers need encouragement. You can't be just a producer of encouragement, nor should you be just a consumer of it. In my final conversations with Mike, I knew he

was discouraged, so I tried to encourage him. I tried, I failed, and I am sorry.

"We have no right to keep the gifts He gave us to ourselves." That's an interesting thought. And it ties in with something I said in my eulogy at Mike's funeral, which was before I re-read this article:

> *"I want to honor Mike by giving a eulogy that is eloquent. But I can't do that because when God was handing out the oratory skills, he gave them all to Mike. I got none. And you know what? I am okay with that because my brother put those skills to good use. Better than I would have done. Mike did not waste any of his God-given talents. Instead, he used them all, and not just the oratory, to the best of his ability, helping people and glorifying God. And what better eulogy is that?"*

Also, what Mike wrote about Del could be said, almost verbatim, about himself: "Del [Mike] the art [criminal justice] teacher would be missed by his students. Del [Mike] the singer/songwriter [speaker/writer] would be missed by his fans. Del [Mike] the friend would be missed by his friends. His family, especially his wife [fiancée] and soulmate, would all be left with big holes in their hearts. They would be more like craters that no one else could ever fill." It was almost like he was writing his own eulogy.

In 2016, Mike wrote the following:

I stuck my head in The Veranda tonight in Starkville. While I was there, I remembered that the last set I ever played in a bar was with Del Rendon in 2004. The last song we played was "Your Time is Gonna Come." Eleven months later, Del was dead. He was one of the most unforgettable people I have ever met. Everyone in town talks about him until this day. The reason is simple: Del cared about people, and they knew it while he was alive. Live well, people. Your time is gonna come, too. If you care about people and they know it, you'll not soon be forgotten.

Mike cared about a lot of people, and we will never for get him.

June 29, 2013, Wentzville, Missouri (St. Louis).

CHAPTER 19

Never Underestimate
a Father's Love

Written in 2017, just months after the loss of our father.

In Chapter 7, I wrote about our parents' move to the outskirts of Huntsville, a town not far north of Houston, and how well that worked out. Now, we fast-forward fifteen years to find that they have moved closer to Houston to The Woodlands, a major suburb just north of Houston's city limits.

There were several reasons for this move. Dad retired from his job in Huntsville—his second career, so to speak—and so now he and Mom were completely retired. They were getting older, which meant they were having more health concerns and wanted to be closer to their doctors. Moreover, they no longer had the energy to maintain their nine-acre property, so they sold it and bought a house with a very small yard.

It worked out well for everyone. It was a nice house, and Mom turned it into a warm home, as usual. They were happy there. Mike and I enjoyed our visits. I always slept like a baby in their guest bedroom. It just felt like home. Mike liked the area so much that he seriously considered The Woodlands for his future retirement home. So, as much as we enjoyed their home in Huntsville, we also came to enjoy their home in The Woodlands, which we assumed would be their final home. But then, this happened...

I have a lot of conversations with young people who complain of a broken relationship with one or more of their parents. After listening to their concerns, I always take the time to tell them about the last disagreement I had with my father while he was still alive. It's impossible to hear that story without realizing that we don't fully understand our parents until they are gone.

In December of 2013, I went home to The Woodlands, Texas to see my parents for Christmas. I didn't know that it was going to be a rough visit until my dad asked me to go into his office to speak privately. Those private conversations with Dad were infrequent but they never turned out well. On this occasion, Dad was telling me that they had decided to sell the house and move into a retirement community.

I was not happy to hear the news. I loved that house and hated to see them sell it. But even more than that I hated to see the beginning of the inevitable march toward the end. The move from the house to the retirement community was just a first step in that march. Next would be the move from the retirement community to the nursing home. And from there, the next move would be from the nursing home to the cemetery. No one wants to get started down that path.

That day, I was bothered by more than just my dad's decision. I was also bothered by his resolve, which I thought crossed the line into belligerence. When he announced his decision, Dad looked me straight in the face and said, "Son, I know this new place will be expensive, but I don't give a damn. I want to live my last years in luxury. I hope I die as soon as I've written my last check emptying my bank account. I certainly don't care about leaving anything to my children."

I was shocked to hear my father say that. It wasn't because I needed any of his money. I started preparing for retirement long before he died *[me too]*, and I am not at all concerned about my finances. It was just the belligerence I could not handle. His tone seemed pointlessly harsh.

I could not make sense of it. Later, I called my brother to share my concern about the way Dad had acted. *[I remember that, and I was also disconcerted.]* But nothing would make sense until my final conversation with my dad, which was three years later.

I will never forget that last coherent conversation with my dad as he was dying of cancer. His weight had dropped down to 120 pounds and his eyes were sunken in his face as he calmly looked at me and said, "Son, I am not afraid to die. All I want is for someone to take care of my wife."

During that conversation, Dad calmly explained the financial arrangements he had made for Mom in anticipation of his passing. Finally, he directed me to a drawer where I could access all of his passwords and find up-to-date documentation of all his accounts. I was stunned at his methodical preparation and attention to detail.

It wasn't until after my dad died that I learned three very important things about the kind of man he really was. They follow in no particular order of importance:

First, the fact that my dad never bought anything nice for himself was not because he didn't have money. Dad lived modestly all his life because he wanted to make sure he had put something away to care for Mom in case he died first. He also wanted to save enough so that his kids would inherit something after both their parents had passed.

Second, Dad never really moved into a nice all-inclusive retirement home for selfish reasons. In fact, he would have preferred to die in his own home. But he knew there were problems with their health. Instead of burdening us with his worries, he sold off all his real property, his RV, and his truck to consolidate his finances and make things simple for us once he died. He also wanted a community where people would cook and clean for my mom once he was gone—instead of leaving her with a kitchen and a big house to manage.

Finally, Dad wanted to leave us with the impression that he was spending his savings because he did not want us to expect anything from him. That way, we would worry about our future enough to save for ourselves. He didn't care if it would make us angry with him. He was more concerned about loving his sons than being loved in return.

Earthly recognition meant nothing to Dad, but duty meant everything. That's why he was a great man. Yours might be just as great, even though you might not know it until he is gone.

I am grateful Dad gave us one of the best gifts that a father can give: the gift of self-reliance. Mike and I both worked hard and were successful in our respective careers. We were never on food stamps or welfare. We were not socialists. We were not entitled. We accepted personal responsibility for our own lives. And there is another dimension to this in the sense that Dad's own self-reliance led to yet another gift: the gift of not being a burden on his children in his old age. Thank you, Dad. I am determined to follow your good example.

By the way, Mike is focused on Dad in this article, but Mom was totally on board with all this; they worked together.

One didn't drag the other out of the house. After Dad passed, she was responsible with her finances until the end and carried on the strategy that she and Dad had begun. Also, I appreciated how they downsized in a stepwise fashion. They were not hoarders. They did not leave a mess behind for us to clean up. Conversely, I have suffered from the bad experience of dealing with someone who failed to get his affairs in order and refused to cooperate with his family, leaving a big mess behind. Literally and figuratively. I am determined not to follow that bad example.

Finally, I want to clarify that although Mike wrote about Dad in glowing terms, Mike was not idolizing or glamorizing our father. There is no denying that Dad had his rough edges, and we had our issues with him, but Mike wisely chose to focus on the good because Dad did, in fact, have positive effects on his children—and in the end that is what is important.

*Mike with Jake, the best dog ever, at our
parents' home in Huntsville, Texas.*

CHAPTER 20

━━━━━━━⟨≈⟩━━━━━━━

In the Living Years

Originally published in 2019 as "Life and How to Live It, Part XIII."

Mike and I grew up together but were apart during our adult years, having followed different career paths in different parts of the country. Our lives had gone in different directions but would re-converge as we worked together when our parents entered the final chapter of their lives. This is a period when some families become fractured due to conflicts over health care, inheritances, etc. However, this was a period during which Mike and I drew closer. I am proud of him for his patience and attentiveness during this time. I am proud of us for working well together and doing our best under some very adverse conditions at the end of our parents' lives.

My father died just before the holiday season began three years ago. This story concerns an argument we had during one of my Christmas visits to Houston. I thought it would be good for people to hear it before they spend time with their families over Christmas.

I was planning on visiting my parents in The Woodlands, then visiting friends across town in Katy and then in Clear Lake before circling back to see them again prior to going back to North Carolina. But just as I was preparing for the day trip across town to Katy, my dad began lecturing me on my need for a GPS. I told him I did not need one, as I had been to the Katy destination several times before.

For some bizarre reason, my dad just kept on arguing with me. When my mother tried to change the subject, he kept interrupting both of us until my mother begged him to just shut up. She only told him to shut up when he was way out of line—so that usually worked. But not this time. He just kept going.

Finally, in anger, I looked at him and said, "Dad, there is no problem here for you to solve. So, stop interrupting me!" Before I realized it, everyone was either yelling or angry. I then told him I did not drive 1,250 miles to put up with his nonsense. I grabbed my bags and stormed out of his house, vowing never to visit my father again.

I spent the night in Katy just as I had already planned to do. The next day, I drove down to Clear Lake as I had also planned to do. After spending the day and the early evening with a friend, I decided to just start the drive back home to North Carolina instead of going back to The Woodlands.

I guess I just did not want to face my father again. I was furious at him for lecturing me and for raising his voice to me after I drove all the way across the country to see him. He was furious at me for telling him I did not need his advice. We both felt hurt, and we both felt disrespected. Nonetheless, for some reason, as I headed up I-45, at just the last second, I decided to miss the I-10 exit to North Carolina and instead drive back up to The Woodlands.

When I walked into the house, my dad was sitting by the fireplace. I sat down next to him and pulled out an iPad and started showing him pictures of our old house in Clear Lake, which I had just taken earlier that day. He never apologized for raising his voice. And I never apologized for storming out of the house. I just met him where he was and started talking in order to break the silence. Later, I found out why Dad had been acting strangely during that visit. A massive tumor had started growing in the middle of his brain.

Had I taken that exit and gone back to North Carolina, things never would have been the same again. Instead, I made peace with him. In fact, I was the last person ever to speak to him. I even delivered a sermon to him on his last Sunday on earth, as he lay there blind, mute, and dying. He died peacefully, and I have been at peace with it ever since. It was all because I met him where he was and started talking.

If there is someone you love that you are not at peace with, just swallow your pride and reach out. Chances are the source of your conflict really is not as important as you once thought it was. Perhaps it is just as meaningless as the one between my dad and me. In fact, I'll bet it is.

We are all dying, folks. It is time to meet the people we love where they are and start talking. There is no need to wait until the holidays to start applying this principle. We can start today. We might not have tomorrow.

I am grateful for the wisdom and insights that Mike left behind, and I am sad that there will be no more of these articles. Here are a few more quotes along these lines:

When my father died, we were at peace. But looking back, I have deep regrets about how I rushed our phone calls because I was working or was simply tired from work. I cannot get those precious moments back. That haunts me from time to time. Work will always be there. Loved ones will not.

The best advice I can give anyone is to assume that each call with a loved one is the last one we will ever have. Unless we are taking people for granted, it does not matter whether we know which conversation is the last. Think about it.

Mike at the grave of Dizzy Dean.

One of Mike's Little League team photos.

CHAPTER 21

Hall of Fame

Originally published in 2015 as "Life and How to Live It, Part XII."

Ah, baseball… Mike and I both played Little League. He was very good; I was embarrassingly bad. But we both enjoyed it. Our parents were on a tight budget, but they would still sometimes take us to see the Astros play in the Astrodome ("the Eighth Wonder of the World"). Later, as he traveled across the nation giving speeches, Mike would catch an MLB game whenever he could and buy a baseball cap for his extensive collection.

But this isn't really a baseball story…

One afternoon in early August, I got off a plane in Gulfport, Mississippi with my friend J. Warner "Jim" Wallace. We were scheduled to speak at a church up in Hattiesburg with our other friend Frank Turek. We had about three hours to make the one-hour drive, so we had plenty of time.

As we headed up U.S. 49 to Hattiesburg, we passed a number of small towns in South Mississippi where many of my relatives were born and raised. My parents met in Gulfport back in 1952 and most of my mother's side of the family was spread across the southern portion of Mississippi. I felt sorry for Jim because he had to listen to stories about my childhood memories of visiting many of those relatives in the Magnolia State.

As we approached the exit for Wiggins, Mississippi, I told Jim about the time in the summer of 1973 when I visited my mother's uncle Wiley Trellis "Bud" Myers in nearby Brooklyn, Mississippi. Uncle Bud offered to introduce me to his friend Dizzy Dean, who lived just a few miles south of him in Wiggins. "Come back and stay with me a little longer next summer and I'll take you down and let you meet ole Dizz," he promised me. But, unfortunately, the old St. Louis Cardinals Hall of Famer died in the summer of 1974 just before I made it back to Mississippi.

I told Jim, who is a retired LAPD cold case homicide detective, that Dizzy Dean was buried somewhere nearby. He took out his cell phone and started to search for the location of the grave. When I asked him what he was doing, he said we were going to find the gravesite. "Today, you're finally going to get to pay a visit to ole Dizz," Jim assured me.

After about forty-five minutes of searching (only to find the wrong graveyard), we got back on the highway. As fate would have it, the next rest stop was named after Dizzy Dean. We figured someone there would know where ole Dizz was buried. Sure enough, an attendant dictated the directions while my ace detective/friend Jim wrote them down. We were off to the races again. We still had time to make it to Hattiesburg after paying our respects to an old baseball legend.

Thankfully, we found Dizzy's grave in a little cemetery just yards off Highway 49 in Bond, Mississippi. There was a large headstone with a smaller plaque just a few feet in front of it. The plaque had a St. Louis Cardinals logo on it, and it also acknowledged Dizzy's membership in the Baseball Hall of Fame.

When I looked down, I noticed a baseball sitting in between the plaque and gravestone. I saw that someone had written on it, so I picked it up to see what it said. It was a short note written by a grown man thanking Dizzy for playing catch with him during the summers when he was just a boy. After staying only a few minutes, we got back in the car and headed towards Hattiesburg.

When we drove off, Jim said, "Well, it looks like you finally got to meet ole Dizz." He also reflected on how a man could rise to such greatness and be known around the world just to end up resting in such a little cemetery in the middle of nowhere in South Mississippi. Jim concluded by saying that it just shows how fleeting this life really is. I agreed wholeheartedly.

When we arrived at the church, we had just enough time to grab a bite to eat before heading to the auditorium. As I was passing through the lobby, a woman came up to me and told me she had driven several hours from somewhere in Alabama just to hear us speak. She explained that her son had just seen Frank and Jim and me speak a few weeks before at Summit Ministries in Colorado. She said the experience had a big impact on him, so she wanted to hear what we had to say.

Another woman approached me and said that her son Nathan had told her to say "Hello" to me. I could not remember his face, but she told me I had a big impact on his life. He, too, was once a student at Summit Ministries.

As I entered the church auditorium, a man walked up to me and introduced himself as the provost of a college in South Mississippi. He said we had corresponded several times many years before. He said he had been trying to fight the good fight as a conservative Christian in higher education. He thanked me for writing about that struggle for so many years.

After Frank spoke to the 650 church members who were in attendance at our Fearless Faith seminar, I had a chance to speak for an hour. When I finished speaking, a man came up to me and said he had just become the university attorney at a school not far from where we were speaking. He told me he had been reading my work on campus free speech for years. Then he told me he was actively working with the Foundation for Individual Rights in Education to eliminate the many unconstitutional policies at his university.

As I was walking out of the auditorium, I could not help but think about all the fleeting relationships I had established over the years as a speaker and a writer. I have met so many thousands of people and forgotten most of them over time. But, strangely, through the wonders of an Internet column, many of these relationships were being sustained. And good things were still coming out of them.

Just as I reentered the lobby, I heard someone call my name. When I turned around, I saw it was one of my old college roommates whom I had lived with in the summer of 1988. Standing next to him was one of my old college friends who was now his wife. I had no idea they were married, as I had lost track of both of them over 20 years ago. He said he had been reading my column for over a decade and was enjoying my exploits. We stood there and launched into almost an hour of conversation—just sharing updates on old friends from the Sigma Chi days at Mississippi State.

That night, I thought long and hard about the effect years of travel was having on my life. It had caused me to lose track of many old friends. But it also caused me to meet many new ones. In the end, I realized that it really isn't up to me, anyway. It's just what I am called to do.

After my plane landed the next day in my summer home of Colorado, I drove from the airport in Colorado Springs to Summit Ministries in Manitou. Later, when I sat down at dinner, one of the students sat down next to me and asked me what goals I would need to accomplish before I died in order to conclude that I had lived a full life. I told him I really didn't have any. I've accomplished enough in my life. Although I am healthier than I have ever been and plan to live many years, I told him, I could die tomorrow and be fulfilled. And I really meant it.

The student was surprised by my answer and just looked at me and asked, "So, what do you plan to do for the rest of your life?" My answer was simple: "Just exactly what I am doing now."

The writing and the speeches are great. But the hikes up the sides of mountains talking about life with students and close friends are really more than enough for me. They are about so much more than enjoying God's creation. They are about trying to produce a ripple effect from meaningful relationships with people who care about important things.

I guess there was a time when I thought life was a struggle to make it into the Hall of Fame. Now I know that it's more like a game of catch on a warm summer afternoon.

"I could die tomorrow and be fulfilled." It is a great consolation to me to know that Mike felt that way. And he had good reason to—Mike accomplished more during his 55 years than I or most other people could in 110 years. I will be forever grateful for what he taught me, and so many others, about life and how to live it.

Photo credit: Summit Ministries, Manitou Springs, Colorado.

CONCLUSION

I began this book by pointing out that Mike was a man transformed, and I listed those transformations. In the chapters that followed, I shared articles in which Mike described those transformations in his own words.

But the transformed Mike did not just sit alone on a mountaintop and bask in the glory of his enlightenment. He was a teacher who taught with passion and honesty and courage—and at great personal expense, ultimately costing him his life. By doing so, he positively impacted the lives of thousands of people. You can hear from a few of them in the "Extra Credit" section that follows.

I, of course, was also positively impacted by Mike, and in my narrative, I have already mentioned some of those ways. For example, In Chapter 8, "Everlasting Life on Death Row," I recounted that Mike helped me on my spiritual rebirth, which included getting me to read Mere Christianity. *In Chapter 4, "A Good Father," I mentioned how Mike led me to a better appreciation of our father. Mike was a good son who honored the fifth commandment.*

Earlier, I alluded to my admiration for how Mike never did anything halfway. When he decided to do something, he gave it everything. He wasted little time on distractions and did not allow his space to become cluttered. For example, Mike loved to play the guitar, so when he passed away, he had eight beautiful, expensive guitars in his house.

In that spirit, when Summit Ministries renovated an old building on their campus to become the Mike Adams Memorial Studio for audio and video recording, they didn't just patch it up, quickly throw in some old equipment, and set up a makeshift studio. They went all out, and now, we have a beautiful, state-of-the-art facility that will be spreading the gospel and preserving Mike's legacy for many years to come. Long after his passing, Mike will still be making an impact.

So, Mike's influence is not over yet.

Remember, in Chapter 6, "A Good Mother," he wrote: "I think what Mother wanted for today is for us to acknowledge the reality that death, within the Christian worldview, is an opportunity for rebirth and for rejuvenation. That is the way it was for her. And the fact of the matter is that the idea of rebirth and rejuvenation through death is actually the entire story of Christianity."

Mike's death was a tragedy, but it is still an opportunity. And not just a random opportunity. It is not just by chance that you are reading this. Let's step back one last time to Chapter 17, "Adams v. UNCW," the story of Mike's great victory in court in which he so eloquently described what happened. The end of his speech was so powerful that I thought, "That's how this book should end!" So, I repeat it here:

Your battles are going to be epic. Your struggles are going to be great. But let me tell you something. You're here for a reason. You're not here by chance. You're here because the Lord has been raising you up to do something great since you were little boys and little girls. And this is not chance: this is providence.

Mike, you were indeed a "brave man and good." You are loved and missed.

EXTRA CREDIT

PARTING THOUGHTS

⸺ ❦ ⸺

Here are my favorite quotes from Mike's Facebook page and elsewhere that have not yet appeared in this book.

Life

When a loved one dies, it is understandably viewed as an unmitigated tragedy. But it is also a reminder that someday we, too, will be called home. And that is no tragedy. We were made for another world.

Resentment is like cancer. It will eat you up inside until it consumes your soul. But it is worse than cancer. It can also consume everyone around you.

Never take the bus from the museum complex to Monticello. Walk the trail. This is generalizable life advice. Never take a bus when you can walk a trail.

The next time you feel like firing off a nasty email, pause for a second. Think of someone who does his job well, and fire off an email giving him encouragement. Then go about your business.

I believe in a God of second chances. Otherwise, I would not be writing anything at all or speaking anywhere about anything.

The fifth commandment tells us to honor our father and our mother. It is exceedingly difficult for children to do that when mom and dad are divorced and tearing each other up on social media.

The fifth commandment is one that extends beyond death. It is about more than saying "Yes, sir" or "Yes, ma'am" to our parents while they are alive. It is about living a life that honors our parents even after they are gone.

Last week, I picked up a copy of one of my mother's old Bibles. I just started reading through it. Fortunately, it contains extensive highlighting and numerous post-it notes summarizing her reactions to various scriptures. I am grateful to have the chance to do this. Too few people have such an opportunity, and I will cherish it daily. The commandment to honor our parents does not end with their death.

It is our job to get up each and every day and tell the truth. The fact that people are not listening does not absolve us of our responsibility. The one who refuses to speak and the one who refuses to listen will be judged alike.

Liberty

If a conservative doesn't like a talk show host, he switches channels. Liberals demand that those they don't like be shut down.

According to liberals, rights are not given to individuals by God. They are given to groups by government.

Liberals tolerate bondage so men can be equal. Conservatives tolerate inequality so men can be free.

Is anyone surprised that conservatives want to go back to work, and liberals want to stay at home?

Capitalism works for you if you work, socialism works for you if you don't work.

Socialism is a philosophy that promotes equality by ensuring that no one has anything. That is why it is only favored by those who are either economically or intellectually bankrupt.

Socialism and moral relativism share at least one thing in common: namely, the tendency to destroy any incentive to rise above mediocrity.

One solution to social inequality is to decline to burn down your own neighborhood in response to social injustices, real or perceived. I hate that I have to explain this.

Abortion always kills innocent human beings intentionally without due process. The death penalty rarely kills an innocent human being accidentally with due process. Stop comparing them.

The purpose of the pro-life movement is not to impose guilt over past decisions. It is to impart wisdom over future decisions.

Senator [Kamala] Harris compared ICE to the KKK. Please allow me to differentiate. The KKK was supported by Democrats wishing to keep black citizens from voting for Republicans. ICE is opposed by Democrats wishing to allow non-citizens to keep voting for Democrats.

The new definition of bigot is someone who holds unpopular views and has the courage to defend them.

No one can demand a "right to be celebrated" without infringing on the rights of other people.

If you pay a man to stand in one place and hold a piece of cardboard, then that's what he'll keep doing.

If you want to destroy a great nation, then just undermine the gratitude of its young citizens. Tell them the nation in which they live isn't special. Tell them that for a generation. Then your work is done. They will pass it on to future generations.

People often approach me in public and say, "Thanks for standing up." What they forget to say is, "So I don't have to."

Ideas have consequences. The ideas we express have specific consequences in the course of human history. They may either produce life, or they may produce death among those who hear them.

Jesus did not come into the world to establish government programs that teach people there is nothing wrong with them and that they lack the ability to change. He came into this world to save sinners. But His offer is available only to those willing to acknowledge their sin and willing to change.

And He gives us the power to change, even when talk show hosts tell us we cannot.

And the Pursuit of Happiness

If you have to choose between a woman who smokes and a woman who has cats, pick the woman who smokes. At least there is a chance she'll quit smoking. The cat thing will only get worse.

Waitress: My name is Heidi if you need me.
Response: What is your name if I don't need you?

Person in Starbucks: Every time I see you, you're in Starbucks. Do you live here?
Response: Every time you see me in Starbucks you're also in Starbucks. Do we live together?

My next book will be called "Your Mother Just Sent Me a Friend Request: And Other Things You Never Say in a Biker Bar."

My next book will be called "Your Daughter is Going to be Just as Hot as Your Wife: And Other Things You Never Tell Your Best Friend."

My next book will be called "Your Mother Is Good-Looking: And Other Things You Can Tell a Girl Once But Not Twice."

I'm writing a self-help book for dolphins. It's called the porpoise driven life.

Elizabeth Warren says she is Native American. I have my reservations.

Friend: I agree with you most of the time. Not sure what to make of that.
Mike: I will tell you exactly what to make of it. It means some of the time you are wrong.

Follower: The end is near. Buy now and save ten dollars on my book about Bible prophecy.
Me: If the end is near, why do I need to save ten bucks?

Pastor: Amen!
Feminist: Sexist!

Reader: It must be nice going through your entire life knowing you're always right.
Response: I wouldn't know. I used to be a Democrat.

A gentlemen's club is always devoid of gentlemen. Sort of like a diversity office is always devoid of diversity.

My mother voted republican until the day she died. After that, she started voting democrat.

My spice rack is nearly empty. Ain't it funny how thyme slips away?

Q: Why is a laundromat a really bad place to pick up a woman?
A: Because a woman who can't even afford a washing machine will probably never be able to support you.

Hate mail of the day: "I don't look down on other people like you do."
Response: "Well, I guess that makes you better than me."

There are two kinds of people in this world: those who dichotomize, those who don't, and those who can't count.

The rain is subsiding. The birds are singing. A small strip of land is emerging in my backyard. Isthmus be my lucky day.

In Saudi Arabia, they cut your hand off if you steal a bag of coffee. I think it would be better if offenders were simply grounded.

Congress has just called a joint session to consider marijuana legalization.

Poverty in Idaho is given scant attention. So, I've decided to make a documentary called *Hood in the Boise*.

Jim: Mike, look at that girl. She has cowboy boots. I like her boots. But that means she probably has a horse. I don't want a girl who has a horse.
Mike: Well, at least you know a girl with a horse will be stable.

Jim: What a nice accent. Are you Hungarian?
Waitress: I'm from France. What do you think I sound like... A barbarian?
Jim: I didn't mean to offend you. I like Hungaria.
Mike: Where is Hungaria, Jim? Is it next to Barbaria?

Jim: Let's just go to El Palenque. I like Hispanic girls just as much as I like Irish girls.
Mike: I didn't know that. I need to introduce you to my friend. Her name is Carmelita O'Reilly.

REMEMBRANCES

This chapter opens with words from Mike's dear friend Scott Maxson, whom you met in the first chapter, and is followed by excerpts from the eulogies delivered at Mike's memorial service. It closes with a small sample of the hundreds of condolences that the family received after Mike passed.

Scott Maxson

The Impact of Mike and the 1970 GTO

The high school years can be tough. Having a friend since third grade can really help. Having a friend with a really sweet car, well, that's just an added bonus for a bunch of high school boys trying to be cool.

I remember how lucky I thought Mike was to have a dad who worked his tail off with Mike to build that 1970 GTO into a beautiful hot rod. They really were proud of their work together. I also remember that I didn't have a car and generally that meant taking the bus to Clear Lake High School.

I remember it was about the middle of our junior year, and Mike and I had become a lot closer, going to movies, having Wednesday night dinners out, and of course going to

Bay Brook Mall to shop and check out the girls. Jim Duke and Terry Cohn were also good friends, and the four of us got into all kinds of mischief as well.

Anyway, in the middle of that junior year, Mike and our group were eating lunch in the high school cafeteria, and Mike asked me when I was going to get a car. I said, "I am not sure, but maybe in my senior year." Mike said, "Well I don't want my buddy having to ride the bus to school in the morning, so I will come pick you up on the way." I said, "That would be awesome, but isn't it kind of out of your way to come pick me up in Camino South?" Mike just kind of smiled and said, "Then, I will just have to get up fifteen minutes earlier." That's when it hit me that this guy that I had known since the old days at Whitcomb Elementary was more than just a good friend. Duke and Adams and I were like brothers.

I have so many great memories of cruising around in that car with the guys. Going to football games and especially looking for the after-parties. A lot of times, we would end up on a weekend night heading over to a gravel parking lot overlooking Clear Lake known as "The Rocks." Mike even took the time to teach my sister Lisa how to drive, as the car basically idled at 30 mph and she never had to hit the accelerator. I have a lot more stories here, but I can't share all of those. One thing is for sure—when we rolled in with that 1970 GTO, people would know we were there, and sometimes, Mike may even have revved that engine up a bit to get a little attention.

As the senior year rolled along, we continued to have great times in that car. By then, most of us had our own cars, but we always insisted to go out in the GTO because Mike's car was simply the coolest.

I remember a few years later, the GTO started to struggle with that Houston humidity, and eventually, the rust became a battle as the cancer took over the car. Mike finally had to hang up the keys to that classic car, and we all felt a little sad. However, that began a new chapter of cruising around in another new hot rod, The Grand Am.

None of us will ever forget those times in our lives spent with some of the best friends we will ever have. Mike was a special friend, and to this day, I consider him a brother, miss him greatly, and know how many people's lives he impacted and inspired.

Travis Barham, Alliance Defending Freedom

When Teddy Roosevelt described "the man in the arena," he was not speaking of Mike Adams. But he could have been. For Mike was a man of "great devotion" who "str[ove] valiantly." At times, he knew the pain of failing "while daring greatly." But he also knew "in the end the triumph of high achievement." For he spent himself in the worthiest of causes.

You see, Mike's life showcases the power of God—His power to change a man; His power to use a man.

When Mike came to UNC-Wilmington, he was one of the leftist atheists who fill so many faculty lounges—the last person one would imagine becoming a vocal conservative Christian. So, what happened? Well, God worked.

When the Apostle Paul told us to "be transformed by the renewing of your mind," he did not know Mike Adams. But he knew his Savior, and when Mike met the same Savior, his entire way of thinking was transformed. He started sharing his newfound Biblical worldview—using his irrepressible sense of humor and love of puns. He titled one of his first columns, "The Campus Crusade Against Christ," and the rest is history. Now, no longer was he a magnet for accolades or the rising star in the department.

In 2006, Mike applied for promotion. Not only was he denied, but his chair claimed that he failed in every area: teaching, research, and service. Yet he had not one, but two, Professor of the Year awards hanging on his office wall.

Mike then made a simple, but momentous, decision—to call ADF and insist that UNCW obey the First Amendment. That's when our team began representing him, something I had the honor of doing for the next fourteen years. After filing suit, we uncovered all sorts of evidence university officials had violated the law. They chastised him for his columns. They ignored promotion criteria. The chancellor tried to change those standards to target Mike and then ordered secret investigations of him. They gave him low marks for his teaching without ever watching him teach while he received some of the highest marks from students. They said he didn't research, yet he out-published all but two of his colleagues. They hardly mentioned his scholarly articles but griped long and loud about his columns. And they even allowed someone who falsely accused him of a felony to vote on his promotion bid. All this because they couldn't tolerate someone with different views.

Despite all this evidence, we lost because the district court ruled that Mike's columns, books, and speeches lost all First Amendment protection when he mentioned them on his promotion application. Yet God worked even in that moment of defeat.

We appealed, and the next year, the U.S. Court of Appeals for the Fourth Circuit ruled in Mike's favor, setting precedent that protects all professors. Later, the Ninth Circuit relied on Mike's case to do the same. By taking a stand, Mike set legal precedent that protects thousands of professors in fourteen states and two territories.

But Mike's case was not over. When we returned to the district court, the university was still defiant. At one point, it asked Mike to drop his case, resign, and apologize on the way out the door. Now, that wasn't hard to turn down.

In March 2014—after seven years of litigation and of working every day with people who hated and mocked him—Mike finally got his four days in court before a jury of his peers. Afterwards, it took the jury less than two hours to eat lunch, elect a foreman, and return a verdict in Mike's favor. That moment was unforgettable, especially the sight of Mike in tears at how God had vindicated him and honored his faithfulness with victory. Soon, the court ordered the university to give Mike his long overdue promotion and years of backpay, and that year, UNCW became one of ADF's significant ministry friends!

But Mike would remind us this is not really a story about him. His life showcases God's power. Only God could transform a leftist atheist professor into a steadfast follower of Christ and a valiant defender of truth and then use him to change the legal system, turning defeat into a landmark victory.

When Teddy Roosevelt described the "man in the arena," he observed that our nation's "success or failure will be conditioned upon the way in which the average man, the average woman, does his or her duty, first in the ordinary, every-day affairs of life, and next in those great occasional crises which call for heroic virtues." Mike answered that call with boldness, faithfulness, and humor. This is just part of the reason I will so dearly miss my client, my comrade, and my friend. But nothing would please him more—or honor him more—than for the story of how God led him to follow Christ, stand for truth, and defend liberty to inspire you to do the same. When you do, you will discover—as Mike will soon tell you, making him one of the few to speak at his own funeral, that—no matter the trials or opposition you may face and no matter the end result—you will not be alone. For Scripture tells us that "the eyes of the Lord run to and fro throughout the whole earth to show Himself strong on behalf of those whose heart is loyal to Him."

Frank Turek, Cross-Examined

Giddy up!

That's what Mike would say now. Memorial services are normally somber, but Mike wouldn't want this to be a somber event. This is called a celebration. We're each taking five minutes to demonstrate a different aspect of Mike. I want to show more of his funny side, which was 90 percent of Mike.

My wife and I were sitting on our patio with Mike, and I said, "Mike, do you like corn on the cob?" And he said, "I love corn on the cob. You know, I once dated a girl from Iowa. Yeah. She had a cornfield in her backyard. She turned out to be a stalker."

Then, when his hair started to change, he said, "You know, I'm now a gray rights activist."

And he had the best subtitle of any book I've ever heard, especially a political book; his book is titled *Letters to a Young Progressive: How to Avoid Wasting Your Life Protesting Things You Don't Understand.*

But probably the story that will tell you the most about Mike is a story that he told in our Fearless Faith seminar. Mike, Detective J. Warner Wallace, and I would travel around the country and do a seminar. And who better to have in a seminar called "Fearless Faith" than Mike Adams. I would do the opening, and then I'd introduce Mike. I would put up a bumper sticker that said, "I Hate Mike Adams," and people would wonder, why would you say, "I hate Mike Adams?" And I would say, "Well, the man who made up this bumper sticker, his name is Mike Adams!"

And he would come out and say, "I know you're probably wondering why there's an *I hate Mike Adams* bumper sticker? On April 30, 2009, I went to the University of Massachusetts at Amherst, which is like going into a communist country, and as I'm walking to the building with my host, I see this huge sign that said, "Blank, Mike Adams." It wasn't welcome. It began with an F, and it's a word we can't speak here in church. And so, the host says, "Oh, I'm so sorry."

Mike says, "Don't worry about it. I get it. As I was walking up to the building, I saw a bunch of protesters on the second floor through the glass windows saying, 'I hate Mike Adams. I hate Mike Adams.' So I decided to go up there and join them."

So, he goes up there. And they were all with their signs and pumping their fists. And Mike is up there going, "Yeah, I hate Mike Adams."

Eventually, they looked over at him and said, "It's Satan!" Now, of course, they don't really believe in Satan. They don't believe in evil, but they think Mike's evil, so they asked him what he was doing, and he responded, "I'm about ready to give a speech. What are you doing here?" They told him that he shouldn't be there.

So, he said, "Well, yeah, I saw that sign you put out there." They denied that it was their sign, so Mike asked them who put it out there. Their response: "Oh, that's from the coalition against hate."

As Mike would say, "That's gold!" You can't write or make up anything as absurd as that. The coalition against hate says, "Blank Mike Adams."

Mike asked them which group they were with, and they told him that they were with the Communist Group of the University of Massachusetts at Amherst. And Mike said, "Well, isn't that cute? You're communists." They then asked him to get out of their space. "You don't understand," Mike told them, "You're communists. You don't have your own space. We share space."

Meanwhile, some guy had taken out his iPhone and was filming the interaction. Eventually, it wound up on YouTube. That led to Mike getting a call from a friend of his. Jim said, "Mike, I saw what happened. You know what you ought to do? You ought to make *I Hate Mike Adams* bumper stickers. And when you go to these places, you ought to sell them to these people who hate you, and it will fund your website."

And Mike said, "I did that. It was the ultimate triumph of capitalism over communism."

You know what the ultimate triumph over death is? The resurrection.

So, giddy up, Mike. We will all see you again.

John Stonestreet, The Colson Center

I had the privilege and opportunity to know Mike, to work with Mike, to speak with Mike, and to spend an awful lot of time hanging out with Mike after we spoke. And I loved him. He was a good friend. We spent a ton of time with Mike each and every summer. And we didn't just love Mike; we loved working with him, and we respected the heck out of him.

I'm sure I'm not the only one who waited for his articles to come out and read them fiercely.

With one of two responses:

First: I wish I would have thought of that! or
Second: I can't believe you said that out loud!

Sometimes, it was both responses to the same thing.

He was both a heck of a writer and a heck of a thinker—and that's unusual. There are plenty of writers who can't think and plenty of thinkers who can't write, but Mike could do both, and he could do them really, really well. And I learned a lot about that craft, that trade, that patience from him.

When we told our daughters that Mike had passed away, they cried and cried and cried. I've spent a lot of time since trying to figure out why, what got to them so much. Because they've had loved ones die before. But Mike wasn't a family member. We didn't see him throughout most of the year. Every summer when he was at Summit Ministries, we'd see each other. My kids would go give him a hug. He would come to our home and would come hang out in our garage, and that was the relationship.

We are members of an older church congregation, and some of members have passed away. My kids have been upset—but why did they cry and cry and cry for Mike?

Several years ago, I showed them an episode of *Mister Rogers' Neighborhood*. And at the end of that episode, my oldest daughter, who maybe was five or something like that at the time, looked at me and asked, "Could he see me?"

Mike saw them. He saw those little kids. He saw a lot of us, too, but he saw those little kids. Each summer, he would connect with them. He didn't connect with all of them. He connected with each of them. He connected with each of them in a very individual way, and that is something that I am very grateful for.

Several years ago, I went to see a family that was part of our ministry, and they said, "You know, our daughter is a sophomore at a university, and since she's gone there, she started seeing this guy who is agnostic, and she's walked away from the faith. She has really hard questions. We don't know what to do."

And I said, "Well, have you ever heard of this place called Summit Ministries?" They agreed to send her, and then I said, "Hey, Mike, I want to tell you about a girl that you need to meet." And he responded, "You mean Vivian?" And I said, "Yeah, how did you know?" He said, "We already met. We're having lunch tomorrow."

Over the next two weeks, they spent mealtime after mealtime together, and in Mike's way, being able to just brutally speak the truth when it needed to be spoken and also lovingly look somebody in the eye and see them, he walked with her back to faith.

And that's really a unique legacy.

And it's one that I'm grateful for. Not only is he someone that I want to be like, but also, I'm just grateful that my daughters were able to have that same experience with a guy who had courageously stood up in the ways that Travis just described but could also look a little kid in the eye and treat them as made in the image and likeness of God.

Jeff Myers, Summit Ministries

Mike was not just Dr. Mike Adams to our Summit Ministries staff. They actually called him Uncle Mike. He was the only professor who got to be called Uncle.

I would always tease Mike because he is a year older than me, but he looks younger because I did not wear my sunscreen the way I was supposed to. I would always tease him with the students that he was my younger older brother. And he hated that. So, he told the students, if Dr. Myers mentions my age during graduation, you have to sing "Don't Stop Believin'" by Journey. And I said something about I would thank all the people and I especially want to thank Mike Adams, my younger older brother. I had no idea what kind of trap I had just stepped into. And the students sang "Don't Stop Believin'." Every single word. Which I thought was actually pretty amazing because that song was written when their parents were still in junior high.

I loved how Mike spent time with our summer staff. He dignified every job. He would be there no matter what the job was. They realized, "You know, maybe he is a famous professor, but he's our Uncle Mike. We can do great things, and we can also serve at the lowest level."

When Mike died, it was as if God was saying, "If I were to give you a gift, a co-laborer, somebody who would make every summer fantastic for you and for your fellow faculty members and for your students, somebody who would stiffen your spine, somebody who would chastise you when you needed it but who was always there with a ready laugh and a devastating wit—but you could only have him for twelve years—would you say Yes?" And there's no question that we would absolutely say Yes.

What happened in those twelve years is really extraordinary. One thousand summer staff members personally got to know Mike and be encouraged by him. As did 15,000 young adults. Mike was masterful in the classroom. It was almost like in *The Wizard of Oz*. Mike pulled aside the curtain to show the little man on the bicycle who was running everything. He took away students' fear about going to college. They realized, "I can do this. I can stand for truth. I can 'stand strong.'"

In the last few weeks of Mike's life, as you know, he experienced tremendous turmoil. My wife, Stephanie, and I talked with him and prayed with him through Facetime. He wondered whether or not he had really made a difference. I wished I could have taken the pain away from him because the truth is that he made a tremendous difference. Only in heaven will we know how many babies are alive today because of Mike Adams. Only in heaven will we know how many young people stay strong in their faith instead of straying away because of Mike Adams.

Those who really knew Mike found him to be the truest kind of friend, one who would tell you the truth in love and stand with you whether you agreed with him or not. That is the Mike I will always remember and that the thousands he touched through Summit Ministries will remember.

Scott Klusendorf, Life Training Institute

A colleague of mine writes, "Most people who say they believe abortion is wrong do just enough to salve the conscience but not enough to stop the killing."

That was not Mike Adams.

For the last nine years, Mike had a tradition. He would visit our home around Christmas—almost always Dec. 22nd—on his way to see family elsewhere. Like clockwork, he arrived at 5 PM sharp, and you don't need to guess his opening words:

"Giddy up!"

And boy, did we. My wife, Stephanie, would cook us a great meal, but then, we got down to business. I quickly learned he wasn't stopping by for a casual chat. He wanted marching orders. He had one question on his mind: "What can I do to protect unborn humans?"

We'd go late into the evening, laying plans for his next pro-life adventure. On his first visit, we discussed working pro-life apologetics into his Summit talks and classroom lectures. The next year, we mapped out a pro-life talk for secular universities. The following year, we discussed equipping students to make a case for life at an upcoming youth conference.

After that, he wanted to take the fight directly to those promoting the killing. That meant we spent our evenings doing debate prep. First up was an exchange with Nadine Strossen, the former president of the ACLU. Mike graciously, but persuasively, destroyed her case.

Then, he went after Willie Parker, the self-described "Christian" abortionist. Surprisingly, Parker agreed to debate Mike at UNCW. Mike spent a year and a half studying everything Parker ever said or wrote on the subject. We went over every line of his planned presentation. Mike finished all his prep two months before the event! We rehearsed it all during his Christmas 2018 visit. And it showed during the debate. Mike was in charge from the start. In fact, he knew Parker's book better than Parker did! It was easily the most commanding debate performance I have ever seen!

For example, when Dr. Parker positioned himself as a "Good Samaritan" to women wanting abortions, Mike replied:

> "When someone was found lying and beaten beside the road, you know what the Good Samaritan didn't do? The Good Samaritan did not stop beside the road and slit his throat and slowly and methodically dismember him. I believe the Good Samaritan is a pro-life parable. And I don't appreciate it being hijacked in the name of God."

My friends, that is the heart of a warrior. Our culture hates warriors like Mike because it is sick and twisted. Mike fought on anyway. He wanted to save children. He didn't just feel pity for the unborn. He *acted* like he felt pity for the unborn.

The Bible calls that love.

Love is costly. Sometimes, warriors return from battle crushed from their wounds. I cannot even imagine the weight Mike felt from constant attacks. Nevertheless, he truly loved those humans he tried to save.

If Mike were here today, he'd say, "Don't Stop Believin'." To which I would add, "But believe like Mike did: by acting as if lives depend on you—because they do."

Mike: You soldiered well, my brother. I miss you. December 22nd will never be the same.

Jason Jimenez, Stand Strong Ministries

David, Laura, Marquietta, I cannot begin to imagine the range of emotions that you have been experiencing this past month. Yet I want you to know that, even in your moments of sorrow and anger and despair, God is with you. God is right here with all of us in the midst of our deepest and darkest moments. I want you to know that Mike's fatal act may have ended his life here on Earth, but his life is just now getting started with Jesus in heaven, where there is no more pain, no more depression, and no more loneliness.

That, my friends, is the hope that we have today. Fully knowing that Mike is resting in the loving arms of Jesus. How can we be certain? Because ever since he surrendered his life to Christ in the year 2000, Mike devoted his life to his Savior. Even in his final days on Earth, Mike and I spent a considerable amount of time reading the Bible and talking about his salvation. He had assurance that Christ was his Lord and Savior, and there was no denying that.

One night, after scarfing down several homemade chocolate chip cookies that my wife had baked for Mike, I remember opening the Bible and reading to him these words found in Psalm 32:5: "I acknowledged my sin to you, and I did not cover my iniquity; I said, 'I will confess my transgressions to the Lord,' and you forgave the iniquity of my sin." I then turned to Ephesians 1:6-8, which reads: "So we praise God for the glorious grace he has poured out on us who belonged to his dear son. He is so rich in kindness and grace that he purchased our freedom with the blood of his son and forgave our sins. He has showered his kindness on us, along with all wisdom and understanding."

After reading these words, I looked up at Mike. There were tears rolling down his face. He told me he was so moved with tears, just thinking about how forgiving and loving God has been to him all these years.

Although Mike's final weeks and days were extremely difficult, and the weight of his depression worsened, Mike never took his eyes off of Jesus, the author and the perfecter of his faith.

But why would Mike do what he did if he was looking to Jesus? I don't think you or I can make sense of it all to answer that question sufficiently. But one thing we can openly admit in this room and watching online is that we all suffer. We all have our doubts. And we need to acknowledge that there are many who are consumed with a deep-seated depression that never seems to let up. Even great men of the Bible like Abraham and Moses and Jeremiah and Elijah and the great Prophet John the Baptist all had bouts of depression and suffered from the abuse of others.

Let me say to everyone here today and watching online. There are many things that remain unknown and unanswered.

Even in the final days of Mike's life, Frank, Scott, and myself were there for a dear friend. And together, the three of us have frequently questioned why this happened, wondering to ourselves what more could we have done to help Mike. It's been hard, to say the least. But nevertheless, we take heed. Despite the questions that we all have, despite the heartache that we all suffer with and all the unknowns that we carry with ourselves right now that are in our heads. As I woke up this morning, preparing and looking over this eulogy, I was shocked that I am about to come to this church because Mike is no longer with us. Despite all of that, my friends, we look to the one true and knowable God who will comfort us in our pain while we trust in His faithful guidance into the light of His truth.

Please hear me. Suicide is never the answer. Mike's life was cut short by a deeply sinful and wrong choice, but his life should not be judged or defined by what he did in the end. We are not here to judge Mike based on one horrific decision, but instead, as you have heard from his closest friends today, we measure Mike's life and how he lived based on who he lived it for, and that's what matters. Taking one's life is certainly a loss of continual rewards on Earth but by no means a loss of salvation, and that is where Mike is.

Therefore, I want us to reflect on three amazing qualities of our beloved Mike. These are qualities that he possessed. These are qualities that we have heard already that we loved about him:

Mike was a lover of God's truth.
Mike was a freedom fighter.
Mike was a man with a gentle soul.

In the video highlighting Mike's impact at Summit, he stated these words: "I think we already know who wins in the final analysis. So, what we do between now and then, while realizing the pursuit of justice and virtue and truth, which is intrinsically rewarding, there is no greater joy"—catch this; this is from Mike himself—"there is no greater joy than standing up for the truth."

And boy, did Mike stand up for the truth.

That was a great quality we admired about Mike at Summit. His assuredness in absolute truth and his unapologetic attitude about his faith in Jesus Christ were contagious. Quite frankly, they were inspiring.

My two oldest of four, every summer when we would go to Summit, no matter how many times they'd heard the talks or the giddy up or the puns, they wanted to hear him.

That's how much he meant to so many. He inspired so many. So many young people are living their faith today in all these arenas because of what Mike did and how he lived so well. No matter the challenge, the issue or point of view he encountered, as a freedom fighter, Mike relentlessly stood up for free speech and freedom of one's religion, even if that person's viewpoint ran contrary to his own.

Finally, there's no denying that even in the midst of Mike's bravery, he possessed a gentle soul. The great theologian Jonathan Edwards wrote, "All who are truly godly and are real disciples of Christ have a gentle spirit in them."

Let me tell you that all of us who knew him so well knew Mike certainly had a gentle spirit. Mike was so kind and gracious to people. As you've seen from the dozens of pictures, Mike loved his students, and he sure did love our kids. He once told me that one of his biggest regrets was not being a father. And then, he would say to me, "I love being Uncle Mike."

I think it's safe for me to say, on behalf of all the kids Mike taught at Summit, that they will really miss his big, bright smile, his big hugs, and his corny jokes. These are just some of the great qualities we all loved and admired about our dear friend.

So, as I close, allow me to share these profound words from the Apostle Paul in Romans chapter 14, 7 through 9, to give us comfort and to give us some much-needed clarity. For Paul writes, "None of us lives to himself, and none of us dies to himself, for if we live, we live to the Lord, and if we die, we die to the Lord. So then whether we live or whether we die, we are the Lord's. To this end, Christ died and lived again that he might be Lord, both of the dead, and the living."

Now, at this time, I want to read words from Marquietta. I extend to you on behalf of Marquietta these words she wants to share with you:

Marquietta Braverman

I want to first thank all of you for attending Mike's memorial service today. I know he loved all of you, and you certainly loved him. My name is Marquietta, and I was Mike's fiancée. Like many of you, I, too, was greatly impacted by Mike on so many levels. For years, I had followed him and read every article he wrote. I always admired that he spoke out with such courage and conviction on the First Amendment, religious liberty, and protecting the unborn. His example as a Christian and a pro-life warrior inspired me to get more involved in my church and pro-life causes. That shared passion for defending the unborn is what brought us together. I reached out to Mike for help on a pro-life presentation I was preparing for my church. He was so gracious, encouraging, and supportive. He even convinced Scott Klusendorf to come on board to offer his guidance and expertise.

Through this, Mike and I became friends, and in time, he and I grew closer, and eventually, we fell in love. Mike and I talked a lot about marriage and our future. Fulfilling God's purpose for us as a couple was important to both of us. We quickly realized that purpose would likely center around our shared passion of defending the unborn. Mike was in the process of completing a pro-life book and was looking forward to joining the pro-life speaking circuit full time after his retirement from UNCW.

He supported my dream to start a nonprofit specializing in pro-life displays and signage. In the spring, when we were making all these plans for our future, we were unexpectedly hit with COVID-19. That's when things at UNCW got really messy. We worked together to get through the crazy season we unfortunately found ourselves in. We didn't know how long the trials would last. But as long as we had each other and we looked to Christ, we believed we would make it through it all, refined and blessed at the end.

But that's not exactly what happened. My dream, and one I desperately wanted to see come true, was to marry Mike and be a loving and caring wife to him. Never did I imagine that instead of marrying him, I would have to bury him. I trusted my Lord and savior Jesus Christ. He will see me through the pain and grief. It brings me great comfort in knowing Mike is with Jesus in heaven.

Today, you heard wonderful things about Mike, how he stood for truth, shared his testimony with thousands, fought for religious freedom, and was a mighty voice for the unborn. Mike surely was an ambassador for Christ. Therefore, I implore all of you not to waste your life but to stand up for what you believe in. Do not allow the culture to silence your beliefs.

The Bible verse that Mike would often quote to those weary of the enemy was Ephesians, chapter 6, verse 11, where Paul writes, "Put on the full armor of God so that you can take your stand against the devil's schemes." I pray you will be a witness for Christ, just like Mike was to people all over the world. Thank you. God bless.

By the way, if you want to see the service in its entirety:

https://www.youtube.com/
watch?v=IrmV4oBHHCc&t=249s&ab_channel=SummitMinistries

Condolences

As soon as we lost Mike, the condolences began to flow in. His death was tragic, unexpected, baffling, stunning. In the immediate aftermath, I was struggling to try to make some sense out of what had happened. In those most difficult first few weeks, these kind words were most comforting. And they still are.

But they have also been enlightening. I always knew that Mike was popular, of course. But until I saw these hundreds of messages, I did not realize the breadth of his popularity—nor its depth. "Popularity" can be shallow, but in Mike's case, it was deep because he was impactful. I don't think I fully appreciated

that until I read the many testimonials from some of the countless
individuals whose lives Mike touched so profoundly. I am grateful
to have them and would like to share just a few of them here:

> Professor Adams taught me life lessons
> that will never be forgotten. He was always
> quick to help his students and instilled
> a quest for justice that will stay with me
> forever. He was truly an incredible man
> who fought for change. (Mary)

> Dr. Adams was the best professor I ever
> had. I thank him for all he taught me
> as well as his endless mentorship and
> guidance. I wish I could reach out to
> him now as I start law school—a goal he
> helped me achieve. (Jeanna)

> Mike was the reason that I pursued a
> Ph.D. in Criminal Justice. (Jennifer)

> I took Dr. Adams' class because I wanted
> to be exposed to ideas outside of the
> four walls I'd built for myself. Mike blew
> the whole house up. What started out
> as political intrigue turned into a deep
> mentorship. Dr. Adams took me under

his wing and showed me the importance of tolerance, debate, and the search for truth. He was genuine, kind, and unearthly intelligent. While I will forever mourn the loss of a truly great man, I'm beyond grateful for the blessing of his mentorship. The world is a better place because of Mike Adams. (Natalie)

He showed me compassion and kindness where he really didn't have to but came alongside me at the most difficult time in my life. (Jenna)

Despite the politics, most people don't know Mike's graciousness. On numerous occasions, he met with my son to help and advise and coach him on how to study for the LSAT free of charge. He did this out of the goodness of his heart, never asking what side of the aisle he favored. (Luke)

Dr. Adams met me and gave me a mini speech that, in the moment, I found slightly offensive. After going home, I realized that his speech was to teach me to not let things hold me back from success, even though they are things that I can't control. He also spiked my interest in becoming a DEA agent in order to get drug dealers off the street. Before Dr. Adams, I didn't think I could become a DEA agent; I didn't think I was strong enough. After Dr. Adams, I know that as long as I push forward and view obstacles as opportunities, I can accomplish anything I can set my mind to. I'm going to get my DEA badge in honor of the legacy Mike Adams left in my life. (Amber)

Mike changed my stance on abortion during a seminar and ignited a desire within me to actually take Christianity seriously. (Sam)

Dr. Adams was the only reason I continued in my major after my freshman year. I deeply admired his dedication to his students and his work. (Alec)

Our entire family has been changed for the better by knowing Mike. (Kelly)

He helped me in college, in law school, and once I entered the working world. (Amanda)

Those who knew him knew his profound love and respect for his students. He was what a professor was supposed to be: challenging, provocative, uplifting, and excelled at teaching not only the subject matter but how to reason—not what to think but how to think. (Jon)

Mike Adams was a colleague. He was a gadfly, one that is actually of extreme value and much needed in every campus. Mike fought for strong academic programs, not frill programs that do not add to scholarship or students' success in life. The commercialization and the lowering of academic standards in our universities appalled him. (Moorad)

I got to UNCW as a lazy college student just looking to skate through college while having fun. Then, I met Dr. Adams. We had long talks about the struggles I was having in college. He was always there to listen and talk. (Jordan)

He was my professor in a Criminal Law class, which was the most informative, most interesting, and greatest learning experience I have had. (Wendi)

I signed up for every class I could taught by Dr. Adams. He made a huge difference in my education and life. (Wendy)

I was instantly captivated by the enthusiasm and passion with which he gave his lectures. It was clear how deeply he cared about advocating for truth and justice. (Mallory)

Additional Tributes

Mike Adams' Legacy Is Bigger Than Tweets
by Laura Walsh

https://townhall.com/columnists/laurawalsh/2020/07/28/
mike-adams-legacy-is-bigger-than-tweets-n2573274

In Memoriam: Professor Mike Adams, 1964-2020
by Robert Shibley

https://www.thefire.org/news/memoriam-professor-mike-
adams-1964-2020

Hey Cancel Culture: You Picked on the Wrong Man in Mike Adams
by Dr. Jeff Myers

https://townhall.com/columnists/drjeffmyers/2020/07/25/hey-cancel-culture-you-picked-on-the-wrong-man-in-mike-adams-n2573106

A Year Later, Dr. Mike Adams' Legacy Goes Marching On
by Travis Barham

https://townhall.com/columnists/travisbarham/2021/07/22/a-year-later-dr-mike-adams-legacy-goes-marching-on-n2592910

ACKNOWLEDGEMENTS

Another interesting thing about Mike is that, it seems me, he had multiple social circles—his Houston elementary and high school friends, his Mississippi college friends, his North Carolina cigar smoking friends, his Colorado summer friends, his pro-life advocate friends, and so on. But even though he was always the same Mike, each circle viewed him through their own lens. So, it is not really possible, even if I were a great writer, to fully conform to everyone's perceptions. I have tried to cover all the bases to the best of my ability, but in the final analysis, this is my perception. This means that all shortcomings of this book are mine and mine alone.

I am grateful that Mike's social circles have embraced me and comforted me and informed me and, thus, helped me to make this the best tribute that I, with my limited skills (I am an IT guy and a photographer, not a writer) can possibly make it. Now I cringe knowing that there will undoubtedly be someone I forget to include below. But here goes…

Perhaps I should start by thanking Brian Pillmore and Ken Chase for helping me get this project off the ground; otherwise, I might still be talking about it. But after a great start, I was having difficulty meeting my high expectations, and I needed more help and another pair of eyes. Thankfully, I came across Tori Thacher, who gave me an editorial assessment with many great suggestions, thus improving the manuscript, inspiring me, and putting me on the right path towards the end goal. After great progress, I then got stuck on the finishing touches. That's where Lauren Green and the fine folks at Ballast Books came in and helped me cross the finish line.

There were a number of people who looked at the unfinished manuscript and gave me helpful feedback, and I appreciate each and every one. I'd like to specifically mention my friends Ken Carter and Rich Race because they were the first ones to review my early, messy version of the manuscript.

Mike's oldest friends, Scott Maxson (who contributed to the "Remembrances" chapter) and Jim Duke, have become my friends as well and have encouraged me in the writing of this book and in the whole journey.

Special thanks to Sally Akers Joachim for your photo of Mike strumming his guitar and for your invaluable memories and keen insights.

Thank you, Travis Barham, Marquietta Braverman, Jason Jimenez, Scott Klusendorf, Jeff Myers, John Stonestreet, and Frank Turek, for eulogizing Mike at the memorial service and allowing me to include your words in this book.

I am grateful for Jonathan Garthwaite at Townhall for publishing Mike's articles over the years and for permission to reprint them here.

I always knew I wanted this book to be well illustrated, so I would like to thank Summit Ministries for their photographs, Anna Stonestreet for her the painting of the Incline, Brittany Boland for the memorial service photo credit, Alliance Defending Freedom (ADF) and Bruce Ellefson for the cover photo, and Mom for taking those precious pictures and passing them down to us.

Thanks, Mom and Dad, for everything you ever did for me and Mike.

Thanks to my wife, Laura Adams, for her love and support. She knew this was emotionally hard for me and made sure I paced myself so I would not get overwhelmed.

Finally, thank you, Mike, for these great articles. As I write this, I am struck by the enormity of my loss because I know you would have written many more had you lived to an old age. But I thank God that you did live long enough to tell us about life and show us how to live it.

INDEX